NO PLACE
TO
STAY

A HANDBOOK
FOR HOMELESS OUTREACH

NO PLACE TO STAY

A HANDBOOK FOR HOMELESS OUTREACH

M. Elizabeth Fuhr

Dedicated to all the homeless and at-risk seniors living and dead who taught me so much

M. Elizabeth Fuhr
2851 W. 52nd
Denver, CO 80221
E-mail: mefuhr@aol.com
FAX 303-433-5865
www.eoncity.com/mary

Editor: Marjorie Larney
Cover Design: Andrea DuFlon
Front Cover Photo: John Wright. Self-portraits of formerly homeless seniors: Bernice Johnson, Thomas Familia, and others. All the art in these pages is done by formerly homeless seniors under the direction of artist Roxanne Hills and with grant funds from the Oakland Cultural Arts Division, the Oakland Redevelopment Agency, and the Alameda Art Commission.
Back Cover Photo: Maggie Miller. Elizabeth Fuhr and Lovie Burkes in front of freeway under which Lovie used to live.

Library of Congress Catalog Card Number: 95-090489

10 9 8 7 6 5 4 3 2

Printed in the United States of America

PREFACE

The passion to write this book came from my experiences working for six years with homeless seniors on the streets of Oakland, California. I vividly recall the sight of a confused and hungry elderly woman retrieving a half-eaten Kentucky Fried Chicken dinner from a garbage can. Everything in me said, "This is not right!"

I decided to write in these pages what I learned at St. Mary's Center as we assisted three hundred elderly and near elderly men and women move toward full rich lives. As a worker walking with the homeless person, I soon realized that it took a special approach to give the person the best chance to be housed. I discovered that persons like Lovie Burkes and GC, who tell their story in this book, did not have to stay under a freeway or in the marina but could have productive lives united with their families. I first used this knowledge to be a more effective worker, and then as director of the program I shared and developed the ideas further with my coworkers.

I knew I no longer was satisfied to work individually but wanted to see many workers in the United States effectively assisting one-on-one hundreds of people who are homeless. From this desire came my decision to make available an affordable, simple handbook that would increase the skill and knowledge of those who work with the homeless.

I have an underlying concern about homelessness that is only addressed indirectly in this book in the advocacy training section. My deepest concern is the systemic policies that are causing homelessness to mushroom. In the 1970s a path was chosen to radically reduce the national monies used for affordable housing and to dismantle a social system with a safety net that took 20 years to build. United States major cities now have pockets that look like Charles Dickens' England in *Oliver* or Victor Hugo's France in *Les Miserables*. Prior to the recent celebration of the 50th anniversary of the United Nations in San Francisco, the newspapers wrote of the police trying to remove hundreds of homeless from the streets, because city hall was worried about their image. Regarding the extent of homelessness, it must be noted that homelessness is widespread in the United States. It is found not only in all the major cities but also in the most rural areas.

Joan Chittister, OSB,[1] recently stated: "We must know what path we are on, because if we continue we will surely get there." Will that path be such that our streets will be flooded with homeless people?

How do you respond to the homeless person? I learned how from homeless persons themselves. Homeless persons taught me to see the individual and the situation for what it is. The essence of what the response must be I experienced most clearly when I met a disabled man John who befriended Lovie when she lived under the freeway. John tried to feed and shelter her the best he could (see Chapters 5 and 11) when she could not do this for herself. It is the human heart that in the end teaches each of us the appropriate response as individuals and as a democratic society to our local, state, and national communities.

Because I came with a listening spirit, I learned from John, Lovie, and others. It is this listening spirit, as it is uniquely present in each reader, that I desire to awaken. A listening spirit can reverently see the beauty and strength that is found in the unlikely places of human suffering.

Writing this book came as a sort of surprise to me because I am not a writer. I think my friend Gregory Bergman who became a writer in midlife made me think that it was possible that I could also write. So, as I complete this journey of two years, I have a deep realization that it is only because of the efforts of many individuals that this book came to completion. First, I want to acknowledge the seniors who shared their stories, knowledge, and artwork. I commend especially Lovie Burkes and GC for their courage to share their story of homelessness, which so many find too difficult to voice. Others told their stories, too, Harriet, MH, and some who wished not to be named. I wish to thank the seniors whose privacy is protected by removing identifying characteristics and yet aspects of their experiences can help others. I wish to thank all the seniors at St. Mary's who taught, loved, and created in me this book that in the end desired to be written.

At St. Mary's the staff, volunteers, and program participants formed truly a community and this book is a community endeavor. In my own international Franciscan community my Denver province supported me financially and spiritually in the long months when I labored on the many drafts. The sisters in the Ludinghausen, Germany, province gave me the start-up monies. Sister Mary Luke Tobin referred me to the Sisters of Loretto who gave funding for me and several seniors to give workshops that provided the basis for the skill-building exercises in the book. The Precious Blood Sisters of Dayton, Ohio, also donated grant monies for the chapter on the special needs of homeless senior women.

Lynette Lee, the director of East Bay Asian Local Redevelopment, creatively and enthusiastically moved the project forward by introducing me to Jose Arce of Citibank. It is through the generosity of Citibank that the first 1000 copies are printed. I owe a big thanks to Lynette Lee and Citibank. Their support made this book affordable to the homeless worker who is usually underpaid.

Without Marjorie Larney's wholehearted volunteer work as editor this book would have never happened. Marjorie was also my teacher, coach, and most of all my friend. Through Marjorie, Sarah Spangler and her mother Louise Spangler donated my first computer and printer. Jody Rea, Joshua Simon, and Francis Kihanya volunteered their skills to bail me out when I got stuck early on with the complexities of the computer. My Franciscan sisters, Kathryn Leahy, Leona Card, and Agnes Gunther—my high-school English teacher—all lovingly read drafts and gave comments.

Whenever I asked, people freely offered their skills. Photographer and artist Mary Phillips selected and prepared for publication the senior artwork. Artist, Andrea DuFlon designed the wonderful cover and gave consultation. Laura Carstensen, Ph.D., between her busy international studies, gave great support and consultation. Gretchen Blais gave comments on the chapter on addiction. Elizabeth Turner, GG Greenhouse, and Zenobia Embry Nimmer each read the manuscript and wrote reviews. Donna Maynard, SNJM, gave hours of skilled proofreading.

My mother Etta Fuhr's death brought grief, but her support for the project made me also hang on. During this difficult time, Maria Bennett assisted in the word processing. Marta Obuchowsky and Mary Catherine and Bruce Green rescued me with *generous* loans of computer time and skills to bring the project to fruition.

I wish to thank Susan Werner, the present director of St. Mary's homeless senior program, for believing with me in the dream of helping the homeless in ways that aid the body and the spirit. Her creative community effort with the seniors has made it possible for us to continue to share this project.

Maureen Duignan, OSF, gave me daily support listening to the ups and downs of this long journey. My family was always interested in the progress of the project.

I thank each person and the Spirit that brought us all together to fulfill this dream.

TABLE OF CONTENTS

INTRODUCTION ENVISIONING CLEAR GOALS

CHAPTER 1 REACHING OUT

CHAPTER 2 BUILDING THE BOND OF TRUST

CHAPTER 3 UNDERSTANDING THE WHOLE PERSON

CHAPTER 4 WORKING TOGETHER WITH THE PERSON TO ACHIEVE THEIR GOALS

CHAPTER 5 ADVOCATING AND NETWORKING TOGETHER

CHAPTER 6 INVITING THE HOMELESS PERSON INTO AN EMPOWERING COMMUNITY

CHAPTER 7 SUSTAINING THE MOTIVATION OF THE WORKER

CHAPTER 8 HOMELESS SENIORS

CHAPTER 9 HOMELESS SENIOR WOMEN

CHAPTER 10 THE HOMELESS PERSON WITH ALCOHOL AND OTHER DRUG ADDICTION

CHAPTER 11 THE HOMELESS PERSON WITH A MENTAL DISORDER OR A DUAL DIAGNOSIS

LIST OF SKILL-BUILDING EXERCISES & PRACTICAL TIPS

INTRODUCTION ***ENVISIONING CLEAR GOALS***

A PLAN TO HELP THE HOMELESS PERSON

Under a freeway overpass, a 60-year-old homeless woman beds down for the night on the cold pavement. She first arranges a piece of cardboard on the ground. Then, she slowly lowers her arthritic frame. She wraps herself in a green army blanket. Before she closes her eyes, she peers nervously one last time beyond the freeway pillars to the police station. She prays she will be safe.

Every homeless person has a name. This woman's name is Lovie Burkes. With shy caution, caring passersby sometimes extend a few dollar bills. Lovie usually accepts the money, but if someone talks about taking her to get help at Social Security she suspects harm and flees. When this happens people often conclude, "She wants to be homeless."

How can concerned passersby, nearby church members or the local community center staff help this homeless woman? No human being is meant to live on the street. No person *really wants* to be homeless. Lovie's furtive existence spells danger and early death.

Lovie and other homeless persons can be helped out of the cold to a warm safe place. A worker can learn the skills to bring the homeless person inside. This book is a manual for the worker who wishes to bring stable housing to the homeless person. Lovie herself and a man named GC add a very important part by explaining their experience of homelessness, and how the process outlined in this book rebuilt their lives.

This book presents to the worker a format to successfully assist the homeless person from the street to housing. The worker can borrow from the example of an Olympic athlete such as Wilma Rudoloph. The athlete Wilma had a dream she believed in. She strove for this dream of a gold medal by well-thought-out steps that were practiced endlessly and by sustained motivation. The worker can successfully bring the homeless person to housing if they chart a focused course that answers the following three questions:

- What Is the Vision of the Homeless Program? (Introduction)
- What Are the Steps Needed To House the Homeless Person?
- (Chapter 1–Chapter 6)
- What Is the Source of Motivation for the Worker? (Chapter 7)

If a worker builds a program that contains the answers to these three questions, the program holds the promise of bringing the homeless person in from the cold. *All the answers are not in these brief pages,* but this is a *basic* framework that works. It was the format that evolved when I was director of the St. Mary's Homeless Program[2] in Oakland, California. Here, in six years, 1988–1993, I and my coworkers journeyed with approximately 300 seniors. The majority of these seniors moved from the crises of homelessness toward a steady future.

I have a great desire to share this knowledge with other workers. I want to provide one basic manual especially for new workers with the homeless. This book is that attempt.

Besides providing in the Introduction and Chapter 1–Chapter 7 a basic framework, this book also includes four chapters that speak to the special needs of certain homeless persons. Again, I only attempt to cover some of the foundational aspects. These last four chapters are:

- Homeless Seniors (Chapter 8)
- Homeless Senior Women (Chapter 9)
- The Homeless Person With Alcohol and Other Drug Addiction (Chapter 10)
- The Homeless Person With a Mental Disorder or a Dual Diagnosis (Chapter 11)

The Introduction and Chapter 1–Chapter 7 are a general framework that applies to working with nearly any age group of homeless persons. Chapters 8 and 9 pertain specifically to homeless seniors. Chapter 10 on addictions and Chapter 11 on mental disorders refer to homeless persons in general, with some specific observations as they relate to homeless seniors. Examples throughout the book are from my work with seniors.

What Is the Vision of the Homeless Program?

The Olympic athlete who keeps the picture of the goal sharply in focus creates the possible—makes the dream become a reality. For a worker, to see in their mind's eye the homeless person finally leaving the streets and sitting in a comfortable safe place shapes the future reality. A strong belief that this homeless person can come off the street is necessary to make it happen. If the worker thinks this person is too far gone, is not worth the effort, is too aggressive, or too sick to be helped, the worker cannot be successful in assisting this person. If a worker believes that only a small number of homeless persons can be housed, that worker will only be able to help a few persons.

Formerly homeless persons, who have stable lives now, can—by sharing their stories—give a new worker the vision that homeless persons with all types of obstacles and disabilities *can* become stable. For a worker to visit a drop-in center or a program where many formerly homeless persons are present to share their stories is also enlightening. Workers stay realistic, sensitive, and honest when they listen to coworkers or volunteers who were once homeless.

Envisioning births a result. When the vision of one worker is shared with other workers and eventually the homeless persons themselves, they can labor altogether for the outcome. The clearer the image of the homeless person's coming into a warm home the stronger will be the endeavor.

What Are the Six Steps Needed To House a Homeless Person?

The process from long-term homelessness to suitable housing is precarious. The steps to house the homeless must be carefully selected and skillfully applied by the worker. Only then can the worker succeed in bringing a homeless person like Lovie from the cold pavement to a warm room.

The six steps that the worker can implement to bring the homeless person indoors are:

1. Reaching Out (Chapter 1)
2. Building the Bond of Trust (Chapter 2)
3. Understanding the Whole Person (Chapter 3)
4. Working Together With the Person To Achieve Their Goals (Chapter 4)
5. Advocating and Networking Together (Chapter 5)
6. Inviting the Homeless Person Into an Empowering Community (Chapter 6)

As in most processes, the worker does not necessarily proceed in a straight line from step 1, to step 2, and on to step 6. For example, the worker attempts to do step 3—understanding the homeless person—right from the beginning to the end. The worker may make inroads on step 2—building the bond of trust—by inviting the homeless person into the community of the other formerly homeless persons, which is step 6. When the homeless person sees former acquaintances from the street trusting the worker, they may also begin to have confidence.

What Is the Source of Motivation for the Worker?

Motivation is the horse that moves the cart. To be motivated toward a goal, a person must be moved by an inner desire. The Olympic athlete's love for the sport fuels their drive against great odds. The stronger the desire, the clearer the vision of the goal it enkindles.

Desire has a history unique to each individual. For the worker to review the history of why they want to assist the homeless person renews the desire. Often, the desire grew from a compassionate connection with those who are unfairly and brutally locked out of the system. For me, an unforgettable life experience was my prime mover. The experience occurred when I, with the untested enthusiasm of a 17-year-old, tried to take on a deep spirituality in volumes rather than by steps. This created in me a very deep anxiety. The anxiety grew. Because of my youth, I had no words to explain my ever increasing pain; it was locked inside me.

In the next few years, through a painful trial-and-error process, I found a peace. From the suffering I attained a new level of sensitivity and compassion. I will *always* remember that inner agony. So, when I noticed a homeless man in the streets of Denver, I first wanted to withdraw with a sense of helplessness. But seeing this elderly man—so alone, needy, and shamefaced—brought to my mind my own earlier experience when I entered the convent and felt locked inside myself. I thought he must be experiencing some of the same feelings of deep pain and solitary unhappiness. I had a great desire to help this trapped man.

Every homeless worker—in fact every individual—has a piece of history that brings some connection with the homeless person's experience of being locked out. When this connection is discovered, an empathy is activated that motivates the worker. Along with this motivation the worker brings personal beliefs and values that fuel the worker's desire to help the homeless. The beliefs that moved me to reach out to create the connection to the homeless person are:

I believe that all humans are created equal.
I believe that each person has infinite value and worth.
I believe that in the core of each being including myself is the home of the Divine that is eternal.
I believe that the Divine Person loves each person equally.
I believe that the Divine lives in each person and can speak to me through that person.
I believe that the Divine wants each person to have a full life.
I believe that the Divine speaks to each person, and I need to listen to that person to know what they really want to do with their life.

All my motivation is not altruistic or conscious because I am recovering from codependent conditioning. As a girl I learned to take care of others needs, even ones they should have taken care of themselves, to gain validation. This, too, spurs, me very strongly. Unless I honestly admit my weakness, understand its presence, and rally the support and knowledge to work at my recovery, it undermines my desire for healthy relationships that empower others.

Through prayer, supervision, therapy, and 12-step groups, this co-dependency is transforming itself from a liability into an asset. Even a worker's disability can be the starting point of assisting another struggling human being to successfully walk to wholeness.

Use of Skill Building

Like the Olympic athlete who practiced over and over to be successful, the worker must, through repetition, acquire skills to achieve these steps. How does a worker gain the skills to do these steps well?

In each chapter of this book are skill-building exercises. The skill-building exercises include questions to sensitize the worker to the homeless person's experience and role-play practice of basic skills necessary to assist the homeless person to get housed. These exercises include some questions that a worker can reflect on alone. These exercises, however, are most effectively used as training for groups of workers. One worker can facilitate and adapt the training and questions to the group.

A formerly homeless person who is now stable and is able to share their story clearly should be invited to be present at each skill-building training. This person is the most effective factor in sensitizing and educating the workers.

SKILL BUILDING—Worker's vision and motivation

- ✓ What is your vision of homeless persons being housed?
- ✓ What most keeps you focused on that vision?
- ✓ Do you have difficulty seeing certain homeless persons housed?
- ✓ Was there a special experience that lead you to think of working with the homeless?
- ✓ What are some of the values and beliefs that shape your work with the homeless?
- ✓ What keeps these fueled for you?
- ✓ What are some experiences in your life story that both motivate you to work with the homeless yet could interfere with the success of your work? What safeguards do you have in place?

SUMMARY

To create a successful plan to help the homeless person, the worker must include the answers to three basic questions:

- What Is the Vision of the Homeless Program? (Introduction)
  When a worker learns that it is truly possible to help the homeless, this vision of the goal paves the way to the possibility.

- What Are the Six Steps To House the Homeless Person? (Chapter 1–Chapter 6)
  The worker uses the following six action steps to bring the homeless person to permanent housing:

  1. Reaching Out (Chapter 1)
  2. Building the Bond of Trust (Chapter 2)
  3. Understanding the Whole Person (Chapter 3)
  4. Working Together With The Person To Achieve Their Goals (Chapter 4)
  5. Advocating and Networking Together (Chapter 5)
  6. Inviting the Homeless Person Into an Empowering Community (Chapter 6)

What Is the Source of Motivation of the Worker? (Chapter 7)

The worker must have a strong personal motivation to sustain this difficult work with the homeless person. This motivation and its beliefs and values need to be understood and renewed to fuel the endeavor. Aspects of the motivation that may interfere with productive work need to be understood and transformed into an asset. Education, supervision, a supportive community workbase and personal-growth experiences aid this process.

Besides a basic framework, this book also includes four additional chapters. These chapters include special needs of some of the homeless.

Homeless Seniors (Chapter 8)
Homeless Senior Women (Chapter 9)

The Homeless Person With Alcohol and Other Drug Addiction (Chapter 10)
The Homeless Person With a Mental Disorder or a Dual Diagnosis (Chapter 11)

Though most of the material in the last two chapters refers to homeless persons in general, there are some specific observations about addictions and other mental disorders as they affect homeless seniors.

Skill-building exercises for the worker are included in each chapter. These exercises aim to sensitize the worker to the homeless person's experience and to improve the homeless worker's effectiveness. The skills can best be practiced in groups. A formerly homeless person as cotrainer is an essential part of effective education.

CHAPTER 1 *REACHING OUT*

Outreach—Poem

I look for you,
You locked inside,
but longing to be found.
I look for you,
Before cold, disease, or train
kill you.
I look for you,
because you are me
and I am you: made
by the same Creator.
I look for you
because God in me
looks for you.
And the God in you
longs for safety, food, shelter,
to be recognized,
heard, and loved.
And the God in me
and the God in you
are one, my Sister.
And I weep!

OUTREACH IS AN ABSOLUTE NECESSITY!

Outreach is an absolute necessity because there are many individuals—like Lovie Burkes who slept under the freeway—whose mistrust limits their human contact. Extreme fear forces people to forage for food in garbage cans to avoid contact with others. Their human instinct directs these frightened people—who *expect* assault—to shield their faces with clothing or hair, or to hide in corners. The personhood dims, clouded by an untold terror. The terror is fed by memories of past abusive trauma, by either real or perceived daily threats, and sometimes by extremely delusional, chaotic thinking. All of this is compounded by a lack of resources. A homeless person may feel hunted and withdraw for protection, but by doing so cuts themselves off from the very resources necessary to live.

As I write this, I remember an incident with one of the frightened persons. I remember my feelings clearly:

> It was late in the evening. After enjoying an outing in San Francisco with my niece and her husband, we made our way through the quiet streets to the ferry. In the shadows I spied a thin woman, perhaps in her fifties. From the indications, she seemed to be surfacing from her hiding place to the pleasant summer air. As the shawl dropped from her head I glimpsed her profile. Her right nostril was eaten away as if by some cancer. Stunned, I imagined her solitary journey to reach this point. I shuddered in thinking of her daily struggle and her future.

Barriers To Accessing Aid

Many barriers block people from readily seeking needed help. Some people feel powerless to access the system because of communication barriers of language difference, illiteracy, or dyslexia (a reading disability). Others, weighed down by pride, shame, despair, mental disorders, drugs, or alcoholism can't find a way out of homelessness.

Some homeless persons expect no change. They have given up. They eke out their existence. They seek hideaways and stand embarrassed in food lines once or twice a day. Some of those who have given up are the same people who many years ago—full of hope—immigrated to this country to work hard for a future. With a slow descent into misfortune and sometimes a mental disorder, they lost jobs, relationships, and housing. The belief that they do not have, or cannot, get the right paperwork from immigration imprisons them outside.

I feel that workers should always spend some time reaching out, no matter how many homeless persons come in the door. From my experience, it was only because of outreach that a certain group of people could be helped. Lovie Burkes is a clear example of one of the persons. Lovie used to pass through St. Mary's grounds often but never came into the office. Her world on the streets was hell, but because of her mental disorder she was trapped outdoors. It was outreach that brought her into the program and eventually to stability.

Lovie Burkes' Story

Lovie told her memories of being out on the street.

> I know out there in the rain or snow, someone will follow you ... going to rape you.
> You're scared someone's following you. If you don't give [them] money, [they] knock you in the head. If you got money, you give it to them. And if you don't have any money, they say you should have some.
> I mind my own business. Joe and his sister used to go to Bean Factory every night. They would come and say "I hate you" and show the knife.
> You feel that no one cares. That the world's against you. Makes you pretty bitter. Staying out on the concrete was hard on me. My back used to give me trouble. I knew I had high blood pressure and arthritis. I think I would have died.

A few months after Lovie came in off the street, she had a large life-threatening tumor removed. She *would have died* if she had stayed on the street without care.

GC's Story

The story of a homeless man named GC gives another example of how outreach is necessary. Early one morning, a coworker and I discovered GC at the marina. GC and his friend were sitting in his friend's car which was jam-packed with stuff. We approached them and struck up a conversation. Eventually, GC came into the program. This is GC's story as told by him.

> I worked all my life [as a carpenter]. But I can't work anymore. After two days with a hammer in my hand [because of my bursitis] I cannot move the arm. [So soon I had a] lack of steady work. You know the grapevine. The word gets around: "GC's arm or leg is giving up on him. He has to take time off." For so many years you're in demand. [Now] "we don't need you. You may have a heart attack. And we are going to have to pay benefits."
> Never in my wildest thought did I think I would be here. It was like the light[s] went out.

> I lived for five years in my truck. [The truck was towed when] I was in the jail for warrants—nothing serious, all misdemeanors—like sleeping in an unwarranted area. It would cost $1800 to get it back [so] I lived under a truck.
> Applying for GA (General Assistance[3]) was so depleting. No one wants to help you out.
> Trying three years to get food stamps. [Only later when his trust was built up did GC share that ...] My barrier was not being able to read [and the] fear that goes along with it. [And again even later did he learn this was a reading disability called dyslexia.]
> Learned to know basic survival tools—rolled up cardboard—best thing to keep [the] bottom warm.

GC, who is 56 and has permanent housing after eight years of foraging, shares his story and does peer outreach to the homeless now. He is passing on the good he received to others. GC says, "It would be wrong after being helped, not to help others."

WHERE TO FIND HOMELESS PERSONS

To do outreach, a worker needs to know where to search out the homeless. This seeking out is necessary, because the most vulnerable—the mentally disoriented, the elderly, and women—strive to hide or blend in to protect their dignity and personhood.

With no place to stay of their own, homeless persons stay in public places: parks, streets, libraries, stores, city buses, local trains and their stations; labor-pool rooms; lobbies of hospitals, airports, and bus stops; doorways; along transportation ways—train tracks, freeways, and bridges; and along waterways—riverbanks, marinas, and beaches. For example, one senior woman went frequently to a clothing bank to receive clean clothes so she would blend in with the public, because she lived for months in the San Francisco Airport passenger terminal.

Homeless persons also may live in private places: their own car or a deserted vehicle, deserted or vacant houses, shacks, boxcars, trucks, factories after hours, caves, fields, hills and forests. (Compiled with the aid of Lovie Burkes, MH, GC, and other seniors who used to live in these places.)

HOW TO RECOGNIZE A HOMELESS PERSON

Homeless persons often try to blend in. The alert worker needs to look for clues or indicators that a person is homeless. The worker guesses a person is homeless—if the person is:

- Sitting near a car filled with clutter and parked at the same location day after day.
- Lugging a large, worn, carrying bag jam-packed with belongings.
- Wearing unmatched layers of clothing for protection from the elements.
- Wearing a shirt with a dark perspiration ring around the collar or other signs of old clothing worn for a long time.
- Wearing rundown old shoes as a result of walking as the only means of reaching different locations.
- Wearing a stocking cap or piece of headgear for warmth at night.
- Wearing a winter coat worn even on a warm day for warmth at night.
- Pushing shopping carts overflowing with clothing and belongings.
- Loitering in the same area for long periods.
- Stashing a tarp, pellets, cardboard, and basic survival tools in ways that look unobtrusive.
- Walking with sagging shoulders and dragging feet out of shame.

Homeless persons leave their nightly resting places and go get food very early in the morning so other people will not know where they sleep. Sometimes, homeless persons are the only ones out on Sunday during the daytime in downtown areas.

IS OUTREACH TO THE HOMELESS PERSON EFFECTIVE?

Our experience at St. Mary's is that with the right outreach, enough time, follow-through, and resources, most people choose to come in. It is a tenuous path that challenges both the homeless person and the worker. The worker needs to pass on to the homeless person the belief that there are other options than living outdoors. The worker needs much skillful caring to go through the stepwise process to assist a homeless person to leave the street and obtain housing. Lastly, the worker needs an extraordinary amount of patience and perseverance.

SKILL BUILDING—Reaching Out

- ✓ Invite a formerly homeless person who lived outside to share their story of survival, and how they overcame the barriers to gaining access to aid.
- ✓ Where have you seen the homeless?
- ✓ How do you recognize them?
- ✓ Have you been surprised to find out someone was homeless that you did not think was?
- ✓ Have you ever felt locked out of a system from some goal you had in life?
- ✓ What were your barriers?
- ✓ What were your feelings?
- ✓ What are ways you coped?
- ✓ What other experiences help you get in touch with the experience of a person living outside?

SUMMARY

Outreach to homeless persons is absolutely necessary because some homeless persons are unable to come to the office because of a mental disorder, pride, shame, addiction, and lack of hope. Sometimes, they experience communication barriers of language difference, dyslexia or illiteracy. Without outreach, the harshness of being outside endangers their lives.

The outreach worker must go to the public and private places that homeless persons use for shelter to find them, for example, transportation centers, libraries, and so forth.

The outreach worker needs to recognize the visible clues that the person is homeless, for example, the shirt with a dark perspiration ring, worn shoes, the stocking cap, and a long winter coat.

Our experience at St. Mary's is that if the outreach worker practices skillful caring with persevering patience, a majority of homeless persons can be stabilized.

CHAPTER 2 ***BUILDING THE BOND OF TRUST***

THE IMPORTANCE OF THE RELATIONSHIP

Building the bond of trust with the homeless person is at the *heart* of the worker sojourning with a homeless person from isolation to housing. *This bond of trust opens the door for all future changes.* Therefore, this step requires the most attention.

I call building the relationship "wasting time." The fox in Antoine de Saint-Exupery's classic *The Little Prince*[4] calls it "establishing ties" and "taming."

The process of relating is simple, mutual, sacred and universal. All human beings have some lonely spaces in their lives. The homeless person has a large lonely space. The door is locked because of their fear. Lovie Burkes (see Chapter 1) in her story called it, "Minding your own business." Every person, even the most isolated and frightened, craves contact. When a homeless person sees a friendly face or receives a warm greeting, this can awaken the desire for "taming" and cause the person to open up the door. The handle to the door of relationship always stays on the inside. Every person controls their own door.

To build trust with a homeless person, the worker must provide careful, patient outreach. The worker must slowly invite the homeless person to open the door of relationship ever so slightly. It means the worker must overcome the barricades the homeless person built against the outside world. These barricades include: shame of being homeless, years of disappointments, loss of self-esteem, loss of contact with families and friends, the terror of a mental disorder, and many others.

In addition, the very state of being homeless demands of the homeless person the single most powerful survival tool—*wariness.* The special vulnerability of a woman or a senior makes them practice even more self-protecting caution. The bond of trust that the worker forms with the homeless person slowly opens this door of isolation and terror. The process from first encounter to the goal of empowerment in the community can only proceed forward if the bond of trust is well-established.

WELCOMING

The worker needs to create a welcoming space in a busy schedule to be truly a warm host to a homeless person. Welcoming the homeless person is so important because it counters the usual daily message received: "No room for you" and "You do not qualify." Homelessness creates dehumanizing experiences. MH, who once was homeless, reported that he saw riders on a bus jeer at those who were standing in line for food. J, who became a coworker at St. Mary's, related how the police would single him out as he rested in the park during the day. They would nudge him awake with their black-booted foot and order him to "Move on." The worker as an antidote to all these wounding experiences acknowledges the person. Once the worker learns the person's name, they greet the person by name.

On the Street

In outreaching on the street, the approach of the worker to the homeless person proceeds uniquely. The encounter begins slowly, carefully gauged to the response. If the homeless person is extremely cautious or confused, the worker proceeds very slowly to make the connection. The worker might just walk by for a couple of days showing a slight interest. The worker might sit on a bench, close enough for the homeless person to become accustomed to their presence.

During all my outreach work Saint- Exupery's story *The Little Prince* served as my model. Saint-Exupery, in the tradition of Aesop and C.S. Lewis, uses the interactions of animals and humans to speak to deeper truths. In this story, the lonely and frightened fox asks to be tamed by the prince so they can be friends. This delicate coming together of the fox and the little prince describes well the bonding process for the worker and the homeless person on the street.

Below is an adapted reading from *The Little Prince*:

Reader:	There is this little prince who comes from a small planet and visits the planet Earth. The prince is lonely and wants a friend. He sees a fox.
Prince:	Will you be my friend?
Fox:	Me? I am a fox. You have to tame me first.
Prince:	What does "tame" mean?

Fox:	It means "to establish ties." It means then you are not just any little boy and I am not just any fox, but we are unique to each other.
Reader:	Now the fox is *very lonely*. He thinks ...
Fox:	I want this nice prince as my friend.
Fox:	(to the Prince) Little Prince, please tame me.
Prince:	How can I tame you?
Fox:	First, you look at me out of the corner of your eyes from a distance, so you don't frighten me. You don't say anything. Words often confuse things.
Prince:	Yes. Then what do I do?
Fox:	Well, you come at the same time every day to feed me. You let me know ahead of time, because half the joy is in the anticipation.
Prince:	I think I can do that. Then what?
Fox:	Then, one day you will tame me, and we will be friends.

As I am writing this on a sunny pier in the Oakland Estuary a beautiful black cat who obviously is not homeless, slowly comes to my side and "tames" me. It is a beautiful process. First she invites me to pet her by relaxing by my feet. I lean down and stroke her. She then jumps up next to me and drifts several times back and forth across my lap and writing paper, demanding my full attention. For a brief time, she rests on my lap contentedly, as I coo and tell her how beautiful she is. Finally, she is satisfied and sits next to me. She then proceeds to give herself a bath—a very private thing to share.

It is the special process of "taming" and forming a tie, that I kept in mind as I did outreach to the homeless on the street. A worker needs to hold in mind the fear that the homeless person has and the care that must be taken to overcome it.

In approaching the homeless person on the street, for the worker to say "Hi" and comment on the weather is a safe way to test the waters. If there is no response, it is O.K. to pass on until another day.

In trying to strike up a conversation on the street, I introduce myself. "I'm Liz. I work at St. Mary's." (I point to the church.) "Do you see that church with the two steeples? Have you ever seen the place? (If the person responds comfortably, I go on to explain further.) We have a program there to help seniors find housing. Do you have housing?"

For those who are homeless and are not frightened, I've found that a relaxed, friendly approach in which I look straight in their eyes with respect and openness, brings a like response. Some people right then will immediately say that they need housing. Some are willing to start working on their future from that moment.

I reveal my name *first*. This relaxes the other person before I ask their *first* name. Some people feel too threatened to share their last name. For example, after three years of visits by our workers, one homeless man on the marina still says, "Just call me 'Joe'." His formerly homeless friends relayed that his actual name is very complex.

The worker needs great *patience* and strives to match the pace of the homeless person. It is a patience measured in years rather than months. A question that guides the pace of the worker is, "Does the homeless person feel comfortable?" When the worker does some action that frightens the homeless person, previous gains in trust are reversed two-fold. Moving too slowly rather than too fast is a safer course.

Once the homeless person shares a first name, it lessens their loneliness for the worker to recognize the person by their name. For the worker to catch someone's eye before voicing the greeting of their name on the street reduces the danger of startling them. Quick movements or reaching out to shake the hand or touch someone on the street easily threatens persons traumatized or mentally disoriented. To others a handshake denotes respect.

A crisis, such as a freezing night, may cause a previously reluctant homeless person to be open to help. Or on a specific day, a certain mentally disoriented person's thought patterns might be clearer. Therefore, it is important for the worker to respond during this openness in a way that satisfies the homeless person, for example, to fill a request for a blanket or a hotel room. This paves the way for a good future working relationship. The worker's prompt follow-up visits build on this happenstance. Otherwise, the homeless person will soon forget the face of the worker. If the worker comes back in an anticipated fashion—like the little prince—slowly, the homeless person looks forward to the worker as a reliable friend and resource.

I discovered I could make use of the chance encounters with a homeless person I recognized as I walked or drove to an appointment. I would pause and inquire how the person was and in a genuine way invite the person to the office. If I did this a few times a week for several months, the person generally would come into the office and work on their problems. In order to give an example, I share the story of my outreach to Lovie Burkes.

Meeting Lovie

> I noticed Lovie around St. Mary's Center's yard. I speculated that she came there after hours for safe shelter. When I moved toward her, she shied away. Several times I asked her name, and she answered rather surly, "Lovie," and then fled. I often forgot her name because it was new to my memory bank. One day she talked to me. I asked her what kind of food she liked. She said that she liked sardines in mustard. I purchased the delicacy. The next time I saw her near the center I hurriedly stopped the car. In my naiveté—with no preparation—I called out of the window, "I have some sardines for you." Lovie turned and bolted.
> It was a year later before I saw Lovie again. This time I was walking downtown, and I happened upon her. Lovie seemed unusually calm and friendly to me. She asked me if I had a quarter for a bus. I was glad that she finally felt free to ask for anything, so I handed her a quarter. This scenario happened a number of times over the next few weeks. Then I suggested to Lovie that we could help her get General Assistance (GA, see note 3). I invited her to the office.

SKILL BUILDING—Building the relationship

✓ Use *The Little Prince* narrative as a reader's theater. Assign character parts and encourage people to read their part with enthusiasm. Afterwards, discuss whether the play describes how people form relationships. Does the play describe your experience of outreach to the homeless on the street?

✓ Discuss my initial outreach efforts with the homeless woman, Lovie Burkes. Which actions of mine were helpful and which were not? Give a reason for your answer.

✓ Use role play to practice street outreach. Form groups of three: 1) the homeless person, 2) the worker, and 3) an observer. Choose three different types of scenarios in which the homeless person on the street is:

a) quick to respond to help but has a few questions. This person may come inside immediately or in a few weeks.

b) moderately fast to respond. This person may take several months to trust the worker.

c) very resistant to help and very confused and frightened. This homeless person flees easily and will probably take years to stabilize.

After the role play each participant reports their feelings. To report feelings use "I" statements, such as: "When you did or said ..., I felt ...."

Rotate roles. Build on the positive and don't forget to laugh.

In the Office

The dynamics of welcoming the homeless person in the office is different from welcoming on the street. The worker might accompany the homeless person to the office for the first time. Or, if the homeless person is not ready to come along with the worker, the worker might just invite the homeless person to stop by sometime. In the latter case, the worker alerts the receptionist that this new person may show up. They ask the receptionist to notify them the minute the person arrives. With homeless persons who are easily discouraged, their appearance in the office might be a one-time trial.

A warm and helpful greeting by the receptionist and then the worker sets the tone. This "red carpet" treatment conveys the message "You are an important person and this agency is concerned about your needs."

Sometimes a homeless person with special needs comes into the office. Frequently the receptionist must clarify services. In a case where the person is seeking services the agency does not provide, the person needs to be referred to another agency.

For those who can tolerate a short wait if the worker is not readily available, the receptionist offers the person coffee. The receptionist lets the person know the time when the worker will arrive. When the worker is able to see the homeless person, they warmly relay the message "I am glad you came."

Lovie's First Visit to the Office

Lovie's first visit to the office reveals some of the special needs of those who have lived outside for a long time:

> She refused coffee. She said, "It might have poison in it." She spoke angrily about the dangerous characters on the street. I gave her my full attention. I feared that she might turn and run. I introduced her to a few coworkers. I noticed that though she was African-American, she responded with fear and aggression to the other African-American women. I took Lovie to the Drop-in Center. Here she met old street buddies. She felt comfortable. In a few days she was hanging around the Drop-in Center, drinking coffee and eating rolls with her buddies.

GC's First Visit to the Office

GC's story shows another example of how a person came to the office after an outreach visit on the street.

After my coworker and I met GC at the marina and invited him to the office, he did not come immediately. I then met him again in downtown Oakland. I repeated my invitation to come to St. Mary's. I reminded him that we had housing resources. GC described recollections of his first visit to the office:

> It was three or four weeks later. It was a cold and rainy night and someone had just stolen my bedroll .... It was hard to come in. I got an extra amount of pride. You laid

> out the services. I came to test the services. If they were not the way you said, I would have said "Good-bye."

When GC initially came to the office his mindset was one of being easily discouraged, and he did not have the patience to wait long for help. Any delay would have said to GC, "We don't want to help you."

Setting the Tone

For the worker to start with an offer of food is a safe bet. Food warms hearts and eases the hunger that dulls concentration.

The worker during the initial interview with the homeless person explains the services and—very importantly—sets the tone. The initial introduction of the program at St. Mary's Homeless Senior Program went as follows: "We help seniors who are homeless or who are in danger of being homeless. In our program here, we will work with the person to achieve their goals. If the person has a problem we can work together on it. It is up to the *person*, what will happen. Then when the person has things going well for themselves, we hope that they will help out others who are new here." This explained the general goal of the program. It keeps the responsibility in the hands of the homeless person and yet offers support. It dignifies seeking services because after the person is able to meet their own goals, they are asked to assist others.

LISTENING

Please Listen to Me—Poem

I don't look you in the eye;
 I'm ashamed,
 but I see you.
Oh, you heard what I said!
You heard that I am hungry.
Do you hear the pain,
 the pain I don't even know,
 the anger at having to ask, to grovel?
Do you know that one day in the 5th grade
 my teacher said I "had the makings of an artist"?
Do you know I raised four fine children
 (though one is dead now)?
Do you know I was a porter for 15 years
 on the Southern Pacific?

Do you know I was a well-thought of foreman
of a construction crew?
Or I was a fireman for 20 years?
Do you know I had my own beautiful home
at one time and entertained silk and vested folks?
Do you know I am
more than I appear?
For God's sake
see the real me!

Building the bond of trust is the *heart* of sojourning with the homeless, but the *key* to that step is *listening*. To listen is to love.

To listen to Lovie says:

Lovie matters.
She is important.
She is a valued person.
Her story is important.
Lovie is worth the worker's time.

When the worker listens, this reflects real respect for the person. The listener's quiet openness encourages trust and invites the person's story. In peer training, GC shared his own experience of listening. He said, "If you listen long enough, a person will tell their whole story." Listening with reflective comments guides the conversation smoothly forward. Questions, on the other hand, tend to jar the speaker and feel intrusive.

I remember this incident at St. Mary's when it was absolutely necessary for me to just listen:

> A senior man could not get his Social Security, because he was very private and could not tolerate questions. For several months I went at prearranged times to a winter shelter, said "Hello" to him and listened.
> By listening I learned 95 percent of what was needed on his application. Then when it was necessary two months later to ask him his father and mother's names, it was a small crisis. But because the trust was there, after a knowing hesitation, he smiled and answered.

SKILL BUILDING—Reflective listening

✓ Practice using reflective comments rather than direct questions. Examples of reflective listening:
Example A:
Newcomer: "I found it difficult to go to the Social Security office."
Worker: "Going to the Social Security Office is not easy for you."
Avoid a question, such as: "Why is it difficult for you to go the Social Security Office?"
Example B:
Newcomer: "I am really upset about having to ask for help.
Worker: "You found it upsetting to come here.
Avoid a question, such as: "Why do you find it upsetting?"

✓ Write the following statements on the board and solicit a variety of reflective responses. Add other statements of your choosing.
a) I don't know if you will believe what I've been though.
b) You will think I am stupid for having lost my rent monies.
c) I am terribly upset about my landlord evicting me.

✓ Form groups of three: 1) the homeless, 2) the worker, and 3) the observer. Role play an initial interview using reflective statements. Take turns, sharing feelings as you go. Build on the positive.

During the initial interview avoid interruptions. If a call from a doctor or Social Security is expected, warn the person ahead of time. An explanation why the pending calls must be accepted and an apology for the interruption helps. Through this kind of care the worker conveys the message, "You and your needs are of primary interest to me."

This story of listening shows how in a single interview without interruptions the bond can be sealed:

> A very intelligent, articulate senior who acknowledged she was "crazy" about collecting junk appeared in the office. She had earned a professional salary all her life

> and was now retired. She owned a number of properties. The house she lived in was stashed with junk. It no longer had electricity or plumping. She squeezed into a bed in the rear. She was upset because the city was threatening to put a lien on her house to pay for cleaning up the junk in the yard. She talked for three hours straight. In the end she still had the junk problem, but she realized that St. Mary's cared. After that we had friendly follow-up conversations that lasted five to thirty minutes. But the bond was formed. I felt very hopeful that if she wanted help in the future, she knew a place to come.

A good listener offers openness, a nonjudgmental acceptance, empathy and a respect for the individual's boundaries.

When the homeless person tells a story which discloses a particularly sensitive issue, their antennae are alert for signals of a dreaded rejection by the worker. It is critical for the worker to convey an empathetic presence to the painful disclosure. The worker needs to listen so closely that the words resonate within.[5] This creates for the homeless person a sense of companionship that validates their vulnerable experience.

To listen well is a skill, an art, that bears learning and relearning. Every skill just like piano playing, exacts 15 percent talent and 85 percent practice.

An annual communication workshop would equip workers with new listening skills and brush-ups on the old. Many self-help books contain listening skills that call for mutual drilling with a friend. (It will probably boost the relationship.)

SKILL BUILDING—Listening skills

- ✓ Watch a movie video with the sound turned off. What do the expressions tell you about the feelings of the actors? What does the appearance tell you about the characters? Guess at this as a group. Then, listen to the program with the sound turned on. Discuss the power of nonverbal communication.
- ✓ As a group, complete endings for the following sentence, "When someone listens to me attentively and compassionately, I feel ...." Continue until the group runs out of new ways to complete the sentence.
- ✓ A leader who is also the timekeeper, invites people to divide into groups of three: 1) the speaker, 2) the listener, and 3) the observer. The listener gives only nonverbal feedback, like, eye contact, a nod, and so on. The speaker has two minutes and completes the sentence, "I am happy when ...." At the end of the time, each person in the group shares their feelings, using "I" statements. Then, the leader has people rotate roles and repeat the exercise, till everyone has a chance to do each role. The leader has everyone repeat the exercise this time using the statement, "I feel sad when ...." In the end, the leader invites the group to discuss what they learned from this listening exercise.

LEAVE THE CONTROL AND THE PROBLEM WITH THE OWNER

When the worker respects the homeless person's boundaries and lets them know they have control, it gives them a sense of safety. Remember the fox warned the little prince not to get too close. The worker conveys in word or action, "I am not going to do anything you do not want." This respects the need of the person for control of their own life.

Similarly, when the person expresses a specific need for a piece of clothing or something to drink, the worker needs to attempt to meet that need according to the desired specifications. For example, attentiveness to the person's personal desires and control can be as simple as asking, "How do you like your coffee, with sugar or cream?" This respect for the person's desires goes a long way in making them feel comfortable.

Who Is in Control?—Poem

This is *my* life.
  I may come
  as if I want you to fix it.
This is *my* life
  to mess up
  or to fix.
This is *my* life.
I hate it now.
But someday I hope to love it,
  like I did that summer day by the glittering water in the lake.
This is *my* life.

The difficulties that the homeless person carries can be imaged as a heavy plank across their back. Respecting the person's boundaries the worker sets the stage for support; for example, the worker responds, "We are a team and together we can see what resources there are for your needs." This statement is supportive, but it does not take over the person's life. The temptation of the inexperienced worker is to take on the feelings of helplessness. If the worker becomes hooked into a rescue mode, then the homeless person feels even more helpless. The worker needs to step back and look for deeper solutions that will empower real change in the person's life (see Chapter 7).

A worker might detect that the homeless person's clothing is worn and dirty. If the well-intentioned worker voluntarily brings clothing without being asked, this crosses the homeless person's boundaries and ignores their feelings. It might shame the personal pride of the wearer, suggesting, "I think your clothes are terrible." It also sets a precedent for the idea, "You cannot take care of yourself." It dilutes the power of the person. It is far better to listen carefully and if no desire is expressed, to ask, "Is there anything you need?"

The homeless person also might not have good boundaries or might think that manipulation and lying are the only way to get things. If this happens, then the worker might state the limits patiently and clearly, for example, of food distribution or similar resources. This helps the person establish inner guidelines. For the worker to do this in an honest way that does not shame the person allows for a possible bonding relationship later. It is good to remember that people manipulate, when they do not know how to meet a perceived need directly. Of course, if their perceived need is an addiction, it is important that the worker does not enable that addiction.

When the worker is successful in helping the homeless person meet initial needs, a giant step in building the relationship takes places.

FURTHER WAYS TO BUILD THE RELATIONSHIP

Honesty grounds the trust relationship. For example, to set the stage for realistic expectations for housing is essential. Hopes are not raised and later dashed. When a person is obviously manipulating, a simple, knowing smile can often halt that train of conversation. Usually, strong confrontations are left till later in the relationship (see Chapter 10).

If, during the initial interview, it is noted that the homeless person has an emergency health crisis, it is important that the worker who has formed the initial bond accompanies the homeless person to the hospital. This allows the initial bond to continue to form. If the companion is another person, the initial contact is too brief, and the confusion of going to the hospital will break the fragile beginning.

The need for the trust relationship necessitates programs and workers to commit to long-term work situations. Again, fragile contacts are broken if the core workers move on too soon. With any change of workers, the homeless person suffers. Their fragile stability is jeopardized by the smoothest transfers.

When the homeless person new to the program is comfortable, the worker introduces them to the staff and the community of formerly homeless people. This introduction broadens the homeless person's resource base. Dependence on one person is avoided. Even if that worker leaves the program, the homeless person will still come back to the program for assistance.

Finally, there can be occasions when the homeless person is made to wait or is upset by a worker. A good relationship is still possible if the worker does not hesitate to give a sincere apology. No one is perfect. For the worker to admit making a mistake can put the relationship back on track and even move it forward.

SUMMARY

Building the bond of trust with the homeless person is at the heart of the worker's walking with a homeless person to stability. This foundation step, therefore, requires the most attention.

Welcoming and engaging the homeless person on the street begins slowly and carefully—gauged to their response. A model for the bonding process is explained in St. Exupery's *The Little Prince*. Here, the fox instructs the little prince on how to tame him, thus becoming his friend.

When the homeless person comes to the office for help the first time, they need a warm and helpful reception. This "red carpet" treatment conveys the message, "You are an important person. We are concerned about your needs." The receptionist must consider that the homeless person, long disenchanted with service agencies might not be able to tolerate a wait, and might interpret this as, "We do not want to help you."

The key to building the bond of trust is listening. To listen is to love. Listening with reflective comments rather than intrusive questions invites the homeless person to tell their story. To listen well is a skill, an art, that exacts 15 percent talent and 85 percent practice.

At St. Mary's the worker sets the tone. They let the homeless person know the services that are available and that accomplishment depends on the homeless person's determination to work on their problems. Support is lent by saying, "As a team we can work on these problems." The worker dignifies the process by saying that after a person is helped, they are invited to assist the ones who are new in the program.

The worker sees the problems as the homeless person's and lets them know they have control over their life. The worker respects the person's personal wishes and boundaries by asking even inconsequential things, such as, "How do *you* like your coffee?" The worker does not assume the homeless person needs, for example, such things as new clothes but asks the person, "What do *you* need?"

Noting further ways to build the relationship, the worker needs to be realistic about the availability of services. The worker stays with the person if there is a need to go immediately to the hospital as a direct way to build on the initial relationship. Continuity of workers and the connection of the person into a healing community is necessary for success in stabilizing homeless persons.

George Tillman

Photo by Susan Werner

CHAPTER 3 *UNDERSTANDING THE WHOLE PERSON*

I Want To Know You—Poem

I want to know you.
I want you to know
 I respect you.
I treasure each word you say.
When you tell me of your heartaches,
 I remember my aches
 so I can better relate to your aches
 (though I do not burden you with these).
I want to know how you see this world.
I want to know who the real you is,
 the one that the Potter and you
 together are chiseling out in beauty.
I want to know what made our paths cross;
 what sad circumstance led you
 to this day, to not have a
 roof over your head.
I want to know what you—
 the you that knows how to care
 and respect yourself—
 really wants.
I want to know you
 and listen to you;
 because today you are
 the bearer of my Creator coming to me,
 the Creator whom I love.
And today by listening to you,
 I may hear the voice
 of Truth and Love with
 a special message for me.
And I don't want to miss these words
 or this loving gift.
I wish to treasure the gift
 and the bearer.

A PERSON IS A PERSON

Many people, even service workers, pull back at the discovery that someone is homeless. If the lack of shelter mars personal appearance and hygiene, the onlookers might distance themselves further. To deny the possibility of a like fate or the nagging sense of personal collusion, the viewers mentally banish the homeless person to a different planet or species. Or, they might blame the homeless person wanting to believe that they are the sole creators of their situation.

All Human Experience Is the Same

An excellent psychology professor[6] stated that all human experience is the same. Fear, hope, fantasy, delusion, and longing jostle all lives. Only the degree of the disturbance varies. For example, fear gnarls the nerves of a student taking a test, but the level of fear escalates to absolute terror for a homeless woman being raped.

To demonstrate the truth of the similarity of human experience, the professor asked a student to dim the lights. Then he guided everyone to close their eyes and to imagine Louis Armstrong in midstage with his trumpet in hand. He said, "Try to hear that distinctive tone." After a few moments, the professor stated that everyone in the room had just fantasized something that was not real. This fantasizing is no different than the hallucinations of those walking the streets speaking to imaginary enemies. It differs in degree only.

Any worker needs to realize that they can experience the same kind of sensations and feelings as each homeless person they meet. They are simply one person relating to another person. When the worker welcomes the homeless person, they establish a bond as an equal to an equal. They know they can understand the other's world if they listen carefully. They remember their own similar experiences and imagine how increasing the strength of those feelings would affect them. Therefore, anchored by the truth that they and the homeless person swim in the same ocean of human feelings the worker realizes that they can try to understand the experience of the homeless person.

***SKILL BUILDING*—If you were homeless**

✓ Describe (and write down if you wish) a scenario that would lead you to homelessness.

✓ List the losses that you must suffer to become homeless.

✓ Write next to the losses the subsequent feelings and physical effects accompanying each loss.

✓ As a group exercise list everyone's losses and consequences on a chart. Note similarities.

✓ Discuss different ways the homeless person loses access to the system, and the emotional effect on them. How are these limits of accessibility institutionalized? How can your agency make its services more accessible? How would the job description of the worker change? How can your coalition educate itself about addressing the accessibility issues of the homeless?

Jungian Types and the Enneagram

Any educational framework that speeds and enhances individual understanding of the human experience improves outreach work. I found two instruments that speeded my ability to really understand the inner world of the homeless person. These are the Jungian types and the Enneagram. Corporate teams, spouses, college students and spiritual guides also testify that the study of Jung and the Enneagram improve communication and mutual understanding among individuals.

Jung's system[7] outlines eight personality types to describe ways people relate to themselves and the world. For example, Jung claims that people process new information in two opposing ways. Type I (introvert) digests the material internally. This requires some quiet time alone. Type E (extrovert) grasps reactions externally. This demands some opportunity to exchange ideas with paper or others. If the worker is an extrovert and the homeless person an introvert, the worker needs to allow the person time to think thorough options such as housing. A mere three-hour training in Jungian types can equip workers with some knowledge of type differences that will facilitate communications.

From an uncertain ancient source came a system called the Enneagram[8] that denotes a nine-sided figure. This very complex system specifies nine types of people each with a vulnerability overcorrected by "compulsions." A twelve-hour workshop can guide an individual's self-scrutiny to know what "number" fits them. Once a person discovers their number, a whole pattern of information unfolds to understand aspects of oneself and eventually others.

It astounded me that GC brilliantly and intuitively came up with the compensation principle of the Enneagram on his own. He did this by analyzing how he coped with his dyslexia and observing similar behavior in his fellow homeless. GC stated the principle of compensation:

> Everyone has a roadblock. They make one part [of themselves] look better because it is covering up something the person feels bad about. Like one guy, even though he may let his pants and shoes look terrible, may always have a spiffed-up shirt because that part of his body [has a scar and he feels bad about it]. People have one piece of clothing they will not remove.

The Enneagram system explains the individual's overcorrections become the nine types of compulsions. The compulsions are all part of being human and therefore being limited. The worker needs to first apply these types in self-analysis before they use the types to understand someone else. The types can help speed up the recognition of human core motivations.

For example, if a worker meets a homeless man dressed very distinctively in a spiffy suit, dangling jewelry, a feathered hat and cowboy boots, he might be the Enneagram Number Four. Number Four's dress very uniquely to counter deep feelings of rejection and worthlessness. The worker addresses the underlying vulnerability of the person by the positive statement, "You are important. You have a right to food and to shelter. You are worth it." The Enneagram can provide a more direct recognition of a person's deepest blocks.

Jungian or Enneagram types, therefore, can provide windows though which certain aspects of the person can be understood. Studying the commonalties and differences of the complex human being allows people to relate more effectively.

WHAT ARE THE IMMEDIATE NEEDS?

What are the immediate needs of the homeless person? The worker interviews the homeless person—the newcomer—and asks what is needed if this is not already volunteered. Some of the needs of a homeless person might be any of the following: food, water, clothing, sleeping gear, a place to store belongings, soap, a shower, a place to wash clothes, human contact, a listening ear because of inner pain, encouragement, foot attention, refill on medicine, or information to get any or all of these resources.

Having no private place of one's own prevents the homeless person from storing any personal property. Frequently, bedrolls and belongings are stolen or confiscated. For example, early on, Lovie (see Chapter 1, Lovie Burkes' Story) requested a place to store her bedroll, a heavy green army blanket wrapped around with a cord. Carrying it pained her back as her undetected tumor grew.

UNDERSTANDING HOW HOMELESSNESS AFFECTS THE PERSON

Besides good comprehension of human nature, the worker needs to recognize the physical and emotional consequences of the trauma of being homeless. Formerly homeless seniors testify to these harmful effects.

Exhaustion. Peter H., who was 72 and is still homeless, said, "I wish to keep moving so people do not take my things or harm you (sic) for not giving requested money. I cannot do that without being completely exhausted." You may not have a safe place to have a sound sleep for a long time. Peter told about knowing a women who was attacked when she slept.

Distrust. Abuse and broken promises make a person leery. Lovie said, "Guys would, you know, pull at their pants. I was plenty afraid. Plenty got cussed by me. People said I was independent."

Shame. J, a former seaman who was homeless three years, questioned himself, "How could I let myself get this low?" MH, who was homeless, when he was in his 40s in Chicago said, "You may get so nasty (unkempt) that you don't even want to show your face."

Manipulation. MH said, "You are willing to listen or do anything. Strange to say, but like willing to almost go to the gas chamber if you can be put up for the night." A senior woman who used to sleep in her car said, "Some are the conning type. They may be addicted and want funds for drugs."

Depression and Emotional Upset. GC described his feeling, "I just got disgusted. [I said] to hell with it. I am not going to fight anymore. [You get] so confused, [you] don't know which way to turn. I almost came unglued."

Without Goals. GC stated that homeless persons might be in a survival mode—just wanting food, clothing, and shelter. They might not be able to think beyond that.

SKILL BUILDING—Studying effects of being homeless

- ✓ Compare the above list of effects of homelessness to your list of subsequent feelings if you were homeless.
- ✓ Discuss the similarities and differences. Would it be a good training experience to have every worker spend three days in a planned survival course on the streets?

HOW TO OBTAIN ESSENTIAL INFORMATION

Any agency needs certain facts to access services for the homeless person and to keep proper records. During the first meeting at the office, the worker's primary goal is forming the bond, and collecting information is secondary. Therefore, the papers are set on the side and filled in later. When pertinent information has not surfaced during reflective listening, then questions are asked. For example, "In order to help you get housing or General Assistance (GA, see note 3), I need to ask you some information. Is that O.K.?"

When the outreach worker and the homeless person chat on the street, the interviewing process is different. When pertinent facts surface, the worker remembers and writes down this important information. Often, these clues capture truths locked within by severe paranoia or confused thinking. The homeless person may never be able to answer direct questions.

Basic information to acquire funding and housing include the following: name, date of birth, Social Security number if the person has one, place of birth, sources of income, former employment, and military record if the person was in the service. Names of parents and living siblings facilitate some resources. If there is a designated money manager, that name and address or telephone number are essential. Former landlords or board and care managers can shed light on the person's significant history.

The interview form should include a name to contact in case of an emergency. Frequently, the homeless person is estranged from family and resists providing family information. First the worker reassures the person that the family will not be contacted. The worker might explain quite bluntly with some humor, something like, "It is very important to get this information because people do have serious accidents. Now we want this just in case you die, and we certainly don't expect that." The homeless person will usually respond with the name of an estranged family. On the street, this information often only comes later, if at all.

WHAT MADE THE PERSON HOMELESS?

The worker strives to determine fully the reason the person is homeless. This is pivotal. The worker does not directly ask the person why they are homeless, but by listening puts together the picture from the bits and pieces of information. When the worker accurately determines the cause of homelessness, they can address the underlying obstacles to stability. Otherwise, the homeless person gets stuck on the same merry-go-round of defeating behavior. If the worker skips over the analysis process in responding to desperate pleas by the homeless person, the worker builds their work on fantasy and feelings. For example, the worker needs to gather accurate information about the homeless person's previous rental history in order to know information about their payment of rent and care of the property, etc. When the true causes of homeless are pinpointed, then solid solutions can be sought.

SKILL BUILDING—Causes of homelessness

✓ Pair up and role play an initial interview: 1) the worker and 2) the homeless person. Share with each other in turn your possible scenarios of becoming homeless. During the interview, the worker attends with empathy and reflects back key words and feelings to encourage the homeless person to continue to speak. After the role play share feelings. Finally, write down what you think are the other person's causes of homelessness. Share these observations with the person.

Some Causes of Seniors' Homelessness at St. Mary's

Used money on prescription drugs.
Is a "pack rat" and all money goes on storage places.
Has alcohol dementia and does not know how to get benefits.
Drinks and because of unruly behavior lost place.
Brings prostitutes into housing. Was evicted.
Had a stroke and is mentally disabled. Was tricked out of money by prostitutes and drug dealers.
Lost job because of serious diabetes and does not know how to do paperwork to get disability.
Is ashamed of disability and cannot cope with asking for money to pay the rent.
Lets children or grandchildren use place or funds for their addictions.
Has a long history of drug addiction and does not pay rent.
Has a history of a mental disorder and alcoholism. Does not know how to change things.
Lost spouse, has health problems with extra bills, is depressed and cannot find affordable housing.
Is developmentally disabled. Housing was sold out from under and does not know how to get new housing.
Lost housing due to earthquake. Is unmotivated. Does not know how to get affordable housing.
Lost housing due to earthquake. Has a mental disorder and cannot find housing on one's own.
Has a history of abuse by spouse. Is an alcoholic. Continues to pair up with an alcoholic, abusive partner.
Is manic-depressive. Was destabilized by personal and then financial crisis. Uses alcohol and will not take medication.
Has a mental disorder. Learned to survive and does not trust others enough to change situation.
Is paranoid and thinks people are threatening them in particular and continually moves. Is not able to choose to use medication.
Cannot find work. Is too ashamed to ask for GA or does not know how to apply or that they are entitled to receive it.

Determining Why Lovie and GC Are Homeless

When Lovie was comfortable visiting the Center—but still lived under the freeway—I asked her to ride along as I did errands. She talked about things that happened in her life:

> I was in Oakland from '68 to '74 the first time. One day I walked to Berkeley for my GA. I did not have bus fare.

> I had no food that day. I felt myself about to fall. I pulled the fire alarm. They called the MP's and took me to Berkeley Police. I went to Highland Hospital. Then they took me to Napa (the state psychiatric facility) for 3 months. I went to Julia Anderson's Board and Care.[9] I went home [to Youngstown] when my daughter was sick. I came here the last time in '86.

The way that the worker Diane began to learn GC's reason (see Chapter 2, GC's Story) for being homeless was when he talked about trying to get GA:

> I am a carpenter. I can't work. I don't know how to fill out the paperwork at GA for food stamps. I can't see. I don't have glasses. GA is a no-win situation.

The length of time outside may indicate the severity of the obstacles. Lovie was outside most of the last three years with earlier stints of no housing. Frequently, the time of being homeless parallels the time span necessary to turn the situation around.

TO UNDERSTAND THE PERSON IS AN ONGOING PROCESS

Assessing a homeless person's situation is an ongoing process. Grasping an individual's view of the world takes time. The worker's understanding of the person grows as the relationship grows. To probe before the trust is there strains the relationship. The rapport can never be sacrificed for mere information collecting. The restless new worker might lament, "Nothing is happening." The worker needs to remember that relationships, like seeds, sprout only with nurturing and time. The growth cannot be rushed. To stay interested in the individual's concerns inches the process slowly forward.

TO DETERMINE BARRIERS TO ACCESS

Because the worker strives under great limitations of time and wants to teach the homeless person skills, an accurate judgment of what tasks the person can succeed at alone and what ones require assistance is critical. In the past, the homeless person did not succeed in accessing the system. Correct decisions about what tasks the worker should do with the person and what tasks the person, with instruction or support, can do alone, often spell success or failure in getting the person stabilized. The worker accompanies the person to ensure that initial critical steps tasks get accomplished. This provides time to talk and build the relationship and gives the worker a chance to notice how the person reacts in certain situations.

Factors to be assessed in determining the degree of assistance needed are the homeless person's barriers to access resources on their own (see Chapter 1). These include the following: illiteracy, foreign language, dyslexia, inability to state needs because of mental disorders, shame, and mobility problems. Some homeless people lack the knowledge or the mental stamina to confront the complex array of bureaucracy. Some simply need a phone, transportation, or money for fees to access services.

For example, it was crucial that GC's worker, Diane, determined that she should accompany him to the welfare office. Because she did go with him, she was able to access the services for him. She also learned valuable information by noticing GC's reactions at the welfare office. This was before GC trusted her enough to confide his secret about not being able to read. GC later was able to talk about his anxiety at the welfare office.

> "I am a completely different person when I go down to welfare. My palms sweat and I start to shake. I'm afraid they will ask me to read ... [I am afraid] they will look down their noses at me, and think, 'You are dumb. You cannot read.'"

WHAT IS THE SOURCE OF MONEY?

The person's money source opens the door to getting housed and staying housed. To talk about finances, especially someone else's, is tricky. To inquire about another's finances too soon in the interview prompts jitters that the worker may be out to trick the person out of money. It prepares the person, if the worker before asking about their finances, says, "In order to help you get housing, I need to ask you, what your source of income is." Knowing the money source of the person can also indicate what health resources are available to that person.

ASSESSING THE MEDICAL NEEDS

Logically, the health of the homeless suffers greatly. A haphazard life on the street without proper food and liquid, without protection from the elements, and without a place to rest and care for oneself deteriorates a person's body. Colds, flu, infections, scabies and ticks, TB, and feet and leg cramps (from constant walking) are common among homeless persons. The lack of eye and dental care erodes the vision and the teeth. Diabetes, tumors, and high-blood pressure shorten the person's life span. The program which serves the homeless with consistent access to an outreach healthcare team and excellent follow-up medical care expedites total care for the person. For homeless seniors, aging brings more health problems. This topic is included in the chapter on specific senior concerns (see Chapter 8).

To ask the name of the doctor, as a matter of course, surfaces the length of time since a physician was last seen. To ask if the person is on medicine and what kinds proves helpful. The names of medicine often point the worker to the physical, and sometimes, the mental or emotional ailments of the homeless person.

Earl Bennett

HOW TO ASSESS FOR ADDICTION

Because addiction can cause or accompany homelessness, the worker must consider addiction as a possibility. The chief evidence of an addiction is the inability to account for the use of funds. To assess addiction, the worker has in mind the question, "Where has all the money gone?" When the homeless person reports checks lost in the mail or stolen, unwarranted evictions, or past medical bills, the worker must do careful research to verify this lack of funds. The sincere victim readily aids the worker in calling Social Security on a speaker phone. (The speaker phone is a very important tool that allows the worker and homeless person to be on the phone at the same time. This is done with the homeless person's permission and the knowledge of the people being called.). Social Security will report whether the check was mailed and cashed. The signature on the check can also be checked. Procedures for tracking and requesting a second check are explained. A one-time check loss can be authentic, but a pattern usually indicates that the person is trying to use this means to get immediate funds for drugs.

The homeless person who is addicted and is trying to manipulate the worker often presses for quick assistance. The person may become angry if any verification is sought and tries to get the worker to feel bad about careful assessment. For example, if a homeless person reports a unwarranted eviction after verifiable long stability, this could be a true story or a possible slow deterioration into alcoholism. One coworker says, "Listen to your gut."

Those with addictions usually lose touch with relatives because the abuse wears all ties thin. But many homeless persons keep away from their family for many other reasons as well.

If the worker learns that a homeless person has a designated money manager, this indicates that a long history of money problems has usually preceded this arrangement. Social Security requires a money manager for those with verifiable, specific addictions or other mental disorders.

There are many addictions and they can overlap: alcohol, street drugs, prescription drugs, sex, gambling, and codependency (an addiction to helping when it is other's responsibility). In the experience at St. Mary's, any of these addictions can create loss of rent monies.

Because addictions twin often with homelessness, the alert worker watches for indicators without acting suspicious or judgmental. The most innocent-looking little senior woman or soft-spoken man may harbor a covert arsenal of lies and schemes in order to get their drug of choice. Meanwhile they are slowly killing themselves.

At the end of an initial interview, if it was not clear yet whether the homeless person had an addiction, I would ask a specific question. "If you were to get housing tomorrow, what would you say would be your greatest problem to overcome in keeping that housing?" Sometimes the person would say, "I need to stop drinking."

HOW TO ASSESS MENTAL STATE

To determine the mental state of the homeless person, the worker mentally answers each of these questions about the homeless person:

1. What words describes the emotional tone at this time and what evokes it?
2. To what degree is this person's picture of the world aligned with reality? To what extent is what they see, feel, hear, and smell consistent with what other people's experience?
3. What is the clarity level of their thinking?
4. To what degree are judgments sound? For example, if they get their check, would they give it away and not pay their rent?
5. What emotional needs present themselves? If the person is depressed, are they suicidal? Is there a need for immediate psychiatric attention?
6. Is this mental state provoked only by present stress, or does it have a long history?

Assessing for Suicide

If the homeless person alludes to suicide, such as, "Sometimes I wonder if life is worth it ...," or " I am really down and don't know if I can continue," the worker needs to directly ask the person about their intentions.

The worker says, "Are you thinking of taking your own life?" or "Are things so bad that you are considering suicide?" If the person says "Yes," the worker follows up with, "Do you really think you will?" If the person says "Yes, I have a gun and every night I load it; and one night I am going to use it," then, the worker needs to call 911, say who they are and that they are with so and so who is planning to commit suicide. The police will come and take the person to get immediate psychiatric help. (I have not had to do this in my six years of homeless work.)

If the person has made suicidal gestures, such as walking across the street without looking or taking excessive aspirin, these are real danger signs. To the inexperienced worker, these acts may appear as slight but one needs to heed that a person who is seriously depressed may first practice suicide attempts. Next time, the depressed person might take the whole bottle of aspirin. Suicidal gestures are like practices that increase the likelihood that the person will commit suicide. If the person is depressed but really does not plan to act on the depression, the worker guides the person to get proper counseling and support. The worker can give the person the suicide prevention number. Also, it is helpful if the person participates in a support group. At St. Mary's I did not know of any direct suicides except the continuing of addictive behavior that resulted in death.

SKILL BUILDING—Suicide intervention

✓ Discuss times in your life that you, or someone you knew, was depressed.

✓ Discuss times you were part of a suicide intervention in the past, or felt there needed to be intervention and wasn't. What were your feelings and what was the outcome?

✓ Role play in pairs an intervention with a homeless person who is deeply depressed: 1) is the worker and 2) is the homeless person. Switch roles. Share carefully the feelings each person had. Discuss the intervention process.

HOW TO DO CRISIS INTERVENTION

A difficult decision occurs when the homeless person resists medical attention and is borderline in being at risk from a physical or mental condition. The person may resist medical attention out of fear of being locked up or harmed by the medical profession. Telephone consultation with health professionals, if available, can shed light. The worker might decide to call the ambulance against the wishes of the homeless person. When the ambulance does come, the homeless person might present themselves as capable and state a lack of desire for medical attention. If the ambulance paramedics determine the person's situation is not life-threatening, then the worker may have a confidence problem with the homeless person. The worker can simply apologize and honestly say, "I called the ambulance because I was worried about you. I want to do what you want to do. It is your life. I guess I made a mistake."

THE IMPORTANCE OF CONFIDENTIALITY

Confidentiality underlies the trust relationship. Basically, the worker affords the homeless person the privacy they wish. To not share another's information without permission respects legal rights[10] and boundaries. Ordinarily, at the end of the first interview, the worker asks the homeless person to sign a permission form. The worker explains that this gives them permission to share information with the agencies they have just discussed. The homeless person needs to know that an agency's workers are a team and that they work together to achieve that person's goals. The guidelines of confidentiality need to be presented to all workers and taught carefully to volunteers. These need to be reviewed periodically.

GC spoke of the importance of confidentiality relating to his trust of his worker Diane:

> Confidentiality is so important. One day when I knew I could trust Diane and that what I shared was not going to go any further, I told her [about my handicap]. Diane always guarded my secret. She spoke for me when we went to welfare the first time. She never left me so I would be found out. What a person shares is the tip of the iceberg. If a person has [arrest] warrants, [they] don't want to be found out till they are on their feet.

HOW TO LISTEN FOR CONSISTENCY

Frequently, the boundaries of a relationship and urgency of a situation limit the opportunities of the worker to verify information about a homeless person. The best cues to the truth of the person's statements reside in their consistency. The worker asks themselves, "Do the pieces jibe with one another? Does what the person say make sense?" If a worker is wondering if they have true objectivity, it is good for the worker to run the scenario past another worker to see if they think the story is credible.

SKILL BUILDING—Assessment

- ✓ From the narratives of Lovie and GC in Chapter 1–Chapter 3, assess what information you know about each. Answer the mental status questions as they apply to Lovie and GC from what you now know.
- ✓ Role play in pairs initial interviews: 1) is the worker and 2) the homeless person.
  a) The homeless person's Social Security check was actually stolen.
  b) The homeless person is on drugs and lies about a stolen check to obtain free housing.
- ✓ After the role play, each person shares their personal feelings using "I" statements, for example, "When you begged and wept for a room for one night, I felt ...."
- ✓ Open a group discussion in which each worker shares for two minutes their experience of the importance of confidentiality in people's dealing with their private business. Discuss how this would apply to their work with the homeless.
- ✓ A homeless person complains to a worker about the behavior of another homeless person in the drop-in center. The leader asks group members what response they would give and why.
- ✓ A worker shares an initial interview report. The worker states his understanding of the person first. Others in the groups add their insights. Discuss what additional information could be important.

In this chapter, GC talks about his initial contact with St. Mary's. GC courageously agreed to let his former worker Diane recount her initial understanding of him. This gives insight into the process by which the worker develops a total picture of the homeless person. The following is Diane's account:

> His foremost desire was to read and to be self-sufficient to make the system work for him. There was a lot of anger about the system. He had an intense pride. He

wanted help as a full human being. He didn't want to be pitied. He was very nervous. He craved interaction but was scared at the same time. I remember mostly his anger and his defensiveness which was a cover for his fear. I remember I tried to listen to what was below what he was saying, what it was that made him tick. I was trying to hear him on this level and to respond on that level. I wanted to hear from his point of view. Not that the content hadn't mattered, but what mattered the most was, I listened. He really wanted to be accepted and to know I would be there for him. I said, "I don't care what you do, but I want you to be honest." That was the cornerstone of the relationship. It eliminated a lot of the crap. One time he did not show up for a week. I went to his apartment. He did not answer when I knocked. I heard him, so I knew he was inside. Later he shared, "You cared that much, you came looking for me." He was touched. I learned, on the other hand, that I needed to trust. He was an adult.

SUMMARY

The worker learns to see the homeless person first as a person like themselves. The worker becomes sensitive to emotional and physical stress caused by homeless. This sensitivity is increased by a skill-building exercise in which each worker constructs what could be a possible story of their own journey to homelessness. Two tools are introduced, Jung's personality types and the Enneagram that may expedite the workers understanding first of themselves and then the homeless person.

Accurate understanding of the homeless person by the worker is necessary to interrupt the merry-go-round of homelessness The worker through exercises learns to listen attentively, and with openness, compassion and objectivity. The worker like a good detective, notices nonverbal clues and underlying themes.

The worker balances building the relationship with the need to collect necessary information to access resources. The worker responds first to the immediate needs and then assesses physical needs, personal barriers to accessing resources, financial and medical needs and resources, mental state, and addictions. The worker needs to be able to assess for suicidal plans and when necessary do a crises intervention. The worker's relationship must be confidential and the veracity can be noticed by the consistency of the statements and outside verifications where possible. Getting to know the person is an ongoing process. An accurate understanding of the whole person provides a firm grounding for the next step: empowering the homeless person to clarify their goals and to implement strategies to reach them.

CHAPTER 4 ***WORKING TOGETHER WITH THE PERSON TO ACHIEVE THEIR GOALS***

PASSING ON THE TORCH

This chapter reflects the triple scheme of an effective program for the homeless. A successful program flows from the following:

- a vision of the goal that the homeless can be housed
- six well-chosen steps to walk with the homeless to stability
- workers with well-founded motivation that endures

The present chapter reshapes these goals as they *apply* to the homeless person. Revisiting the total framework places everything in clear perspective.

In this book's introduction, a clear vision of a homeless program begins the journey. Six well-selected steps plot the path from the street to housing. These steps are the following:

1. Reaching Out
2. Building the Bond of Trust
3. Understanding the Whole Person
4. Working Together With the Person To Achieve Their Goals
5. Advocating and Networking Together
6. Inviting Into an Empowering Community

In succession, each chapter in this book examines one step. Chapters 1, 2, and 3 portray reaching out, building the bond of trust, and understanding the whole person. The present chapter illustrates the worker's working together with the homeless person to achieve their goals by *empowering the homeless person to clarify personal goals, plan steps, and keep their motivation alive.*

This represents a full circle. The prototype for a worker in a homeless program is the Olympic athlete who has a goal and practices good skills and keeps motivated. When the worker is successful they are able to pass on the torch to the homeless person. With the encouragement of the worker, the homeless person gets in touch with personal goals, shapes effective plans and keeps their motivation alive. The Olympic athlete's striving toward gold and the homeless person's struggling toward a stable future trace *the same path*—seeing their dream, plotting their course and holding to their belief.

This chapter describes how the worker aids a homeless person to achieve their goals. This is demonstrated by a true story. It is the story of the worker Diane at St. Mary's Center assisting GC (see Chapter 1, GC's Story, and Chapter 3).

The Homeless Person's Personal Goals

> ***SKILL-BUILDING*—Defining the goal**
>
> ✓ You as worker can best guide the unsheltered to a goal by finding your own goal. Write down for yourself a goal for either your work, recreation, or personal life. To pinpoint your goals, answer these questions: What aspects in your recent work, recreation, or personal life brought the most satisfaction? What exactly about it was satisfying to you? These satisfying features point you to the chief components of a gratifying future. To explain this further, ask someone in the group to share a personal goal and the answers to the above questions in relation to that goal.

Immediate Needs

When GC braved the office the first time, he carried two concerns: a warm bed and food. While listening to him, GC's worker, Diane, kept in mind the question, "What is it he wants?" This question focuses the energy of the worker and the homeless person. It also says *his needs* are important and that *his needs* determine what happens.

Temporary Housing

When GC came to Diane, she assisted with temporary housing. She arranged for a room in a transient hotel available through a winter voucher program. GC's immediate needs translated into his initial goals. Now that GC had a place, Diane could easily keep contact to continue their work together.

Available Finances

But Diane needed more information to determine how GC could pay for housing after the voucher ended. Diane encouraged him to talk more about himself. She realized that GC had no steady income because his health problems prevented him from practicing his carpentry trade. She wondered about his source of income for housing. The immediate source available was General Assistance (GA, see note 3). The questions to solve GC's finances were: What is his real medical situation? Can he work or does he need to apply for disability?

Identification and Paperwork

While listening to GC, Diane realized that GC's previous denial of GA was based on lack of identification—a common problem for those without a place to store personal items. Diane—new to the system—quizzed coworkers on how to overcome this obstacle. She then asked GC, "Are you a registered voter?" "No," responded GC. So Diane and GC got his identification through voter registration, and also through obtaining a library card.

GC relayed to Diane his fear of welfare with a partial truth, "I cannot deal with the paper work. I have no glasses."

Diane got the GA forms that St. Mary's has on hand. She read the questions to GC and wrote his responses. Armed with the completed papers, they proceeded together to the welfare office. GC was so impressed that Diane was able to get him GA and food stamps that first week.

Confidence from the earlier achievement and his rapport with Diane spurred GC to deal with more of his long-term goals. She asked him, "Why do you get so nervous when you go to GA?" GC said, "I cannot read." Diane listened attentively as GC shared his dreaded secret and the perils of the struggle. "The teachers would put me in front of the class though I told them ahead I could not read .... I was able to get by [as a carpenter] because my partner knew I could not read. He would run down to me the information and he knew I would run with it."

After listening at length to the dilemma and his pain, Diane said, "What do you want to do about it?"

***SKILL BUILDING*—Overcoming paperwork obstacles**

✓ A worker presents an actual situation where they ran into obstacles in getting a homeless person's finances and papers in order. Plan as a group a strategy for how the worker can overcome the obstacles.

"WHAT DO *YOU* WANT?"

"What do you want to do about it?" Diane asked GC. Diane asked GC to zero in on his real dreams. She wanted GC to get in touch with the goal that is unique and integral to who he is. GC's goal was to be able to read. GC's desire to read was a very deep issue for him.

Every person has desires that reach to their core. Every person's *dream* embodies the sacred. I believe the person's dream resembles a well whose ultimate source is God. That unique person's desire and the Divine's desire for this person are one. This idea reflects a traditional spirituality.[11] Surfacing the true goals of a person shapes the basis of job counseling.[12] People do best in work that really fits them.

GC asserted:

> "I want to be able to read so I don't have to depend on the GA. There is nothing that I want more. I applied to the reading course at the local library and have been trying to get into their reading program for the past year. They keep putting me off."

Diane called the library. She reported to GC, "They smelled beer on your breath so they thought you might be disruptive." With GC's O.K. they contacted a different library reading program. GC got an appointment. To learn to read was GC's long-term goal. This goal surfaced once his more immediate needs were met.

Options

To awaken the vision of a homeless person is to open again future *options* for that person. This is necessary because the downward spiral of homelessness closes down alternatives. GC felt trapped economically, emotionally, and physically. He lived in a survival mode. He saw no options for himself. When his immediate needs were taken care of, GC's spirit ventured on to see new possibilities. The actions of the worker empowered GC to picture options that together they might access for him. His world was enlarging.

Desires

Beneath a goal lives a desire. The desire fuels the goal. This is the "fire in the belly." The desire is the passion that stirs the flames. I consider a true desire what God first aspired uniquely for that person.

People embrace many levels of desires from surface wishes to deep, core yearnings.[13] A surface level desire may be to avoid pain. A deeper longing may be friendship. An even deeper level may be to create and have meaning. A still more profound treasure may be a committed relationship. The deepest core may hold a belief that human life is invaluable and has an eternal, unique purpose.

> ***SKILL BUILDING*—Knowing your desires**
>
> ✓ To journey with a homeless person and to look at different levels of desire, a worker must examine their personal levels of desire. This exercise doesn't need to be shared. Use the lines below or add more to list desires that motivate you from surface ones to deeper desires.
>
> Example:
>
> Desires of my life (Rank with the least important first)
>
> | | |
> |---|---|
> | To be pain free | ________ |
> | To have friends | ________ |
> | To be creative (writing, music, and art) | ________ |
> | To have a committed relationship | ________ |
> | To live out of the principle that human life is purposeful and invaluable. | ________ |

Competing desires rival for attention. By weighing the different desires real choices are made, for example, to choose between temporary pain or a life-long goal. To weigh desires and select one by keeping priority of desires and consequences in mind makes for good choices. If the desire to avoid all pain overrides an important lifelong desire, this may result in a sense of betrayal of one's goals. Thoughtful choices direct life directions. Comprehending goals as they stem from desires readies a person to complete the uniquely human act of choosing.

I CHOOSE

Choosing—Poem

I guess we all want
 freedom
 but, gee, it's so big
 and I'm so small.
Choosing?
Me?
What do *I* want?
Oh, the bottle, of course!
She's my lady.
She, I trust
Always there
(Unless you stop my flow of money!)
What is it?
There is more?
I can want more?
Options?
The bottle or
 a room of my own?
There each night?
Friends?
Self-respect?
I can choose these?
Oh, is it *really* my choice?
Can I dare ...?
If I fail ...?
Time is running out?
But you talk of others,
 how things have changed.
You seem to care ...,
 to believe I can ....
Is it possible ...?
I see you are not
 easily fooled,
 no free ride here.
But do I dare
 choose?

GC asserted the depth of his longing to read. "Before I would go to that hole [die], I am going to learn to read. I'll be happy if I can get to read. I want to be independent of the system. There is a world of knowledge out there in books." With this goal in sight, he prioritized his energies and little monies.

"It Is Your Choice. What Do You Choose?"

Once GC determined his desires, his next challenge was to *choose*. Just as Diane assisted GC, the worker needs to repeat, "It is your choice. What do you choose?" This lays the responsibility and opportunity at the homeless person's feet. To see—at this critical point—a person choose their life is to witness a birth. To *choose life* is a marvel!

Frequently, addiction accompanies or causes homelessness. The person yoked by this tyranny of addiction slowly subjugates all principles, all actions to one purpose—the drug (see Chapter 10). Eventually, the person hits a dead end. The fix no longer suffices. A critical point arises. This crisis affords the opportunity for the worker to explore with the person who has hit their bottom, their deeper desires of *their real self.* Old dreams can resurface and spark hope.

However, this is a long journey with many pitfalls. A transformation in a person's life is usually preceded by many mini-choices. The person with an addiction needs to experience that they can desire, choose, and achieve positive changes. To obtain a drug-free life requires repeated small choices. It demands a certain consistency that avoids paths that sap needed energy or divergent roads that lead elsewhere. Each positive choice strengthens the positive life direction. Each negative choice paves the way to the next relapse. A person with an addiction does not turn away from self-destructive behavior in just one visit with a worker.

SIMON

SKILL BUILDING—Role play of goal counseling

✓ Role play using a fishbowl technique. Two volunteers sit in the center of the group and role play: 1) the homeless person and 2) the worker. The worker assists the homeless person to get in touch with their personal goals. The group discusses what they observed.

✓ Divide the entire group into groups of two: 1) the worker and 2) the homeless person. Each group role plays a worker helping the homeless person to surface goals. You can select a situation—one from your work setting (changing names and identifying characteristics to ensure confidentiality) or use the following scenario:

Jim is a 45-year-old Vietnam vet who just got out of the hospital. He has critical liver and stomach problems related to his alcoholism. He is scared because the doctor has said he will die if he does not quit drinking. He receives a monthly VA check. He has lived with friends or outside most of the past five years.

DETERMINING THE GOALS

Diane helped GC to reach his goals. In overview, these goals were:

1. Immediate Needs
2. Temporary Housing
3. Available Finances
4. Identification and Paperwork
5. Healthcare and Employment or Disability Determination
6. Permanent Housing
7. Special Needs: Counseling

Up to this point in this chapter, Diane guided GC through the basic goals (1–4). The process of pinpointing goals shifted as the basic goals were met and deeper goals surfaced. In the remainder of this chapter, Diane moved with GC toward those deeper goals (5–7).

Healthcare And Employment or Disability Determination

General Assistance provides only temporary aid. GA stipulates the person must obtain a doctor's evaluation of employability. Diane arranged transportation for GC's first doctor's appointment in years. This transportation support to the clinic helped because he was very anxious. He thought they might discover he could not read. The doctor confirmed GC's inability to work and prepared a statement to that effect for GA. This doctor's statements was used for the housing application as well.

Diane assisted GC to obtain from Social Security the disability application. Together, they filled out the lengthy papers. She warned him from the start that it might take three years to finally obtain the benefits. She stated that he would probably have to obtain a private lawyer to advocate effectively for the necessary appeals. The legal fees are frequently one-third of the back payments. Because GC's return to carpentry was blocked, he knew he had to apply for disability. When he obtained the disability rating and entitlement funds, he could retrain for a less physical job. This also meant to GC that he must learn to read. At this point, as the book is going to press, GC is just beginning to receive his disability payment, two and half years after he applied.

Seeking Permanent Housing

Diane quizzed GC on exactly what kind of housing he wanted. She explained to him what housing was available. Specific low-income housing may have certain age, disability, or financial criteria. Because GC was 55 and had a doctor's statement of disability, he was fortunate at that time to be able to get HUD priority senior housing. Two weeks later, the age requirement of the building changed to sixty-two. In the senior housing, GC paid 30 percent of his GA income which allowed him to buy other necessities with the remainder.

Loan Fund

Although GC was ready to move into permanent housing, his GA check would not arrive for a week. Also the amount of the check was not large enough for the housing deposit. Diane asked GC if he wanted to borrow from the St. Mary's loan fund and repay it over the next few months.

St. Mary's small revolving loan fund was instituted to provide money to initially stabilize the homeless person. One thousand dollars created the fund, and $600 was added each year for outright payments and unrecovered or long-term loans. The loan fund provides money for emergency deposits and rents, critical items, and birth certificates. The crux of the success in getting the loans returned rests in the trust relationship, proper screening, and the follow-up built into the program. The decisions about who should get a loan demand critical thinking rather than spontaneous feeling. The agreement to lend is based on a strong surety that the money will be repaid; that is, the homeless person has maintained good credit, has a reliable payee (a second person) who agrees to repay, or that the program is the person's mailing address, and their check will come there. The person's being willing to accept money management (see Chapter 10) might be part of the decision to make a loan.

Realism

To know the limitations and obstacles from the beginning helps a person have realistic expectations. For example, when Diane let GC know that one-bedroom affordable housing was not readily available or that the Section 8 waiting list was at least four years long, it helped him to know his options and arrange his plans accordingly.

Special Needs: Counseling

Many times a homeless person needs special treatment for an addiction, a mental disorder, an emotional trauma from past life problems, or the stress of homelessness. The critical resources are very limited and often require strong advocacy. Frequently, the counseling comes later in the process of getting stabilized.

This is how it happened for GC. He worked well with the reading teacher at the city library. When he returned to his apartment to study, however, confusion wiped out the memory of all he had learned. He became very depressed.

Then, he made an important discovery for himself. "I was listening to the radio. I heard a man, a carpenter, who was very successful but it [not being able to read] limited him." The carpenter on the radio program explained that he had the disability of dyslexia. It was like a light going on for GC. "It was me with a different name." Only then did GC learn why he could never read. "No one diagnosed me. I diagnosed myself. I don't believe that people teaching reading did not know about the [disability] tests. I knew I wasn't stupid." He felt cheated that no one had recognized his need from the time he was 5 to 55 years old.

With relief GC now had the name for his reading barrier. But, GC found that to deal with his dyslexia, he needed to address his walls of shame and fear through counseling. With the help of Diane, he arranged for counseling. "I get $299 a month and I spend $40 to go to a counselor, so someday I can read."

Timing

SKILL BUILDING—A time for everything

✓ Reflect on a personal circumstance where you required a certain timing to deal with a difficulty. What was the effect when someone tried to change your timeline? What were your feelings?

✓ Charting time. Draw a line that corresponds to your age. Place a proportional mark on it that represents how long you've worked with the homeless. Using the same proportions draw a line that represents the age of a homeless person you wish to assist. Put a mark on the second line to show the number of years the person has not had permanent housing. What does this tell about how you look at time and how the homeless person may look at time?

Some observers erroneously think that if a homeless person does not immediately jump at any offering of housing it means, that they want to be homeless. A homeless person, grinding away for daily existence, cannot trust changes easily. New visions proceed slowly for the person blind to veteran benefits or safe, affordable housing, fogged by alcohol, or dogged by delusional pursuers.

The worker's sense of an individual's timing and readiness for housing evolves with experience. To watch for clues, drop hints, and connect the person with others who are further in the journey can aid the process. To rush, shame, or badger increases resistance. Sometimes, the person craves the housing but not the responsibilities. Here the worker clearly repeats the choices and says, "It is up to you."

Often, those who are only at risk of being homeless or homeless a short time respond quickly to assistance. Mysteriously, someone who has been outside for many years may just come inside with a simple invite. This leaves the worker breathless! This breath-taking memory sustains the spirit of the worker during the usually long and challenging battles toward housing those long accustomed to the streets.

GC observed that it took him 3 or 4 weeks and a wintry night and a stolen bedroll to draw him to St. Mary's. God and the homeless person alone determine the timing.

The worker's *patience and perseverance* pave the way for the homeless person to be housed. The worker accepts the homeless person's limitations and paces their exchanges accordingly and celebrates tiny steps of progress. In time a sense of mutuality develops. The homeless person begins to see the worker as part of their life. The homeless person refers to the worker by name, anticipates contacts, and may accept transportation for shopping and medical appointments.

Ask "What Next?"

When the worker who is requesting housing or other services makes sure all the papers are complete, this cuts down on delays. The worker stays focused with the theme of *What will happen next?* In a call to Social Security for a lost check, they learn the date the check will arrive and the procedure if it does not. This practice of asking, *"What next?"* ensures the flow of actions.

SKILL BUILDING—Role play to obtain Social Security

✓ Role play a conversation on a speaker phone with Social Security for a check that is reported lost for a week. Use groups of three: 1) the Social Security person, 2) the homeless person, and 3) the worker. Discuss afterward the effectiveness of the telephone call.

HOW TO KEEP THE MOTIVATION FLOWING

After Diane helped GC to open up the world of his dreams, she needed to support his choices. To accomplish life goals requires a lot of work. Only if a person stays motivated will the end be reached. From the point that GC came into the office, Diane let him know that she was on his team. Together, they worked on his goals. Welcoming GC when he arrived and meeting him one-on-one on a consistent basis gave him a sense of solidarity. This teamwork gives the person heart.

Diane helped GC continue to strive for his dreams. Keeping in touch with that inner fire is needed for difficult life goals to be achieved. The core desire—the dream—gives the homeless person the strength to overcome the obstacles.

Diane invited GC to participate in community activities that affirmed his talents and ideas. This participation rebuilt GC's sense of his own capabilities. Being part of an active community of other formerly homeless persons helps keep the motivation alive. People are a great source of inspiration to one another (see Chapter 6). When GC was asked what at St. Mary's helped him most with his motivation, he said, "Alone you can only go so far. You have to have that encouragement."

Who Wants It: The Worker or the Homeless Person?

Often when a worker sees someone hurting very badly, even being self-destructive, the worker may very much want the person to stop this destructive behavior and choose treatment and the housing that can follow. Sometimes, especially with drugs, it may become apparent that the person is not really motivated and that the worker is wanting the treatment more than the person. That will not work. It has to be the individual that chooses. No one can do it for anyone else. A worker can say, "I am very concerned about your health and I would like you to choose good things for the future. You are the one that has to choose. We are here when you are ready. Be sure and come to our groups and don't be a stranger to us." Once the relationship of trust is formed, the clearer the homeless person sees the choice is in their ballpark, the freer the person feels to choose something for themselves.

SKILL BUILDING—Role play with a manipulator

✓ In groups of two take turns role playing the following situation. A woman came in at the end of the month, two months ago and asked for help to get into a detox center. You assisted her, but then you found out that she left the detox center the first of the month when her check arrived. She now returns to your center again toward the end of the month homeless and penniless and repeats her request. After the role play, discuss your feelings.

Creative Strategies

The worker needs to learn to assist the homeless person to overcome many obstacles to go from the street to stable housing. Some of these obstacles are: agency regulations or barriers, limitation or lack of resources, and addictions or other mental disorders. The approach of a successful worker must be one of tenacity and creativity. For example, if housing deposits are needed, the program or a group of agencies can create a resource like the loan fund or money management. Or another example of creative problem solving took place with a homeless man who needed an identification from Motor Vehicle, but his disability required him to add to his real name many other titles. His worker called Motor Vehicle personnel and explained the problem. Together they arranged that he could write the correct name in the required blank and all the extra titles in a margin that did not disqualify the identification form. The flexible approach of not letting these obstacles discourage the worker or the homeless person is very critical as resources get more and more limited. As a homeless worker, I saw myself as that piece of creative dough that expands to make a proper fit between a system made for the masses and the person with special needs. I refused to give up on a person.

Consultation with other workers, programs, and specialists needs to be a normal part of any homeless program. These outside resource persons often shed light on possible solutions to very difficult situations.

Practical Tips to Case Management

This section is a summary of practical tips for the new worker who provides case management.

Resource Directory. Develop a convenient directory of frequently used numbers that can be readily updated.

Referral List. Develop a brief but accurate list of referral agencies for the people that your agency does not serve. If time permits, call the agency before giving the referral. When your agency and another are jointly assisting a person, keep on-going contact so the person is not lost.

Paperwork and Organization. Organization expedites the flow of information and tasks. Get help if you are not good at organizing. Everyone can learn. Try to make reports brief enough to be practical, but thorough enough to be helpful. Include dates, names, and numbers of important contacts for that person. Reports written daily are much more accurate and painless in the end. Use of the computer eases information flow and keeps vital information for reports, grants, and advocacy work.

continued

Practical Tips to Case Management

Emergency Housing. Visit and develop arrangements with local providers, including hotels, so that a range of services is available that meets special needs, especially for the disabled, the elderly, and those with special safety issues. Call ahead or send letters of referral with pertinent information to ease service linkage.

Social Security. Social Security and SSI (Social Security Supplemental Income[14]) and SSD (Social Security Disability) can all be contacted for information at 1-800-772-1213 or the local Social Security Office.

SSI is mandated and partially funded by the federal government. State participation is optional and requires a partial payment by the state. SSI includes financial and medical benefits for those disabled and elderly with no or limited income. SSD is a disability benefit for those who earned a set income. The amount received is based on past earnings. Easy to read, up-to-date information on each program can be requested from the Social Security Administration.

Generally, if a person is receiving more than one of the above benefits any address change needs to be assured for each benefit because each program has its own department in Social Security. Information is not shared between these departments.

You and the homeless person should always record the name of the person you are conferring with so that all follow-up calls can be directed to that person.

Disability Application. Clearly instruct the person on their rights. Each person has a right to food and shelter if they are unable, through no fault of their own, to get it for themselves. Frequently, especially older people resist requesting benefits because of preconceived societal stigmas. Instruct the homeless person in the purpose of the application: to verify disabilities that confirm why they are not able to work 40 hours a week. Most homeless persons are not at ease at revealing weaknesses and histories. I often tell them that it is important not to try to appear more able than they are. Because of shame, people keep to themselves previous hospitalizations, their inability to concentrate or think clearly, or admission of their lack of other human contact. Denials of long histories of alcoholism and drug abuses also have to be broken through. (Note concern in Chapter 10 about helping addicted persons get unrestricted monies that might end up causing their death.) The worker can fill out an SSI Third Party Verification of Disability Form so the worker can include information that the homeless person excluded. Complete medical information documents the disability, and therefore it is necessary that this is available. Working closely with physicians expedites this information .

continued

Practical Tips to Case Management

Disability applications require many follow-up calls to determine their status and to ensure that the process is completed. There may be required medical appointments by the agency overseeing the disability application. The worker and the homeless person need to be aware that attendance at these appointments is essential to receive benefits.

When a person completes the paperwork, sensitively check for accuracy and completeness. This avoids delays. Keep a copy of all important papers of the homeless person on file.

Veterans Benefits.[15] Note if the homeless person has a military history. Contact the veterans office to determine eligibility for financial or medical benefits. Veterans benefits precede use of SSI. SSI covers what is not included.

Pensions. Note if a person belonged to unions and is eligible for benefits.

Legal Assistance. Work with low-income legal services to assist with obtaining benefits.

Keep On Top of the Situation. In each situation, it is important to know at what step of stabilization each person is, and what is to be expected, especially in cases where the person alone cannot stay on top of certain aspects. Thus, if a piece falls out of place, it can be dealt with in a timely manner. Especially, the new worker in a difficult situation is aided by writing down the plan: What are the goals? What are the steps to achieve these goals? List the barriers, options, people that can help, responses expected, and timeline. Repeat the process as needed.

CLIENT PLANNING FORM

List homeless person's goals and steps to achieve these goals. Update as goals change. Note barriers, options, and people who can help with the timeline for goal(s).

GOALS	STEPS	COMMENTS/TIMELINES
Goal 1.	1.	
	2.	
	3.	
	4.	
Goal 2.	1.	
	2.	
	3.	
	4.	

continued

Practical Tips to Case Management

Healthcare. Discuss with the homeless person their healthcare needs. Emphasize the critical information they need to relay to their physician. If the person has limited ability to share their medical history or the nature of an ailment, an appropriate communication system between the worker and the physician must be devised. The worker may communicate with the doctor by actually escorting the patient, by a phone call, or by a written report. Indicate to the doctor clearly the reasons for the homeless person's visit, for example, a complete physical because of severe stomach pain, verification for a disability application for Social Security, a statement of disability for housing priority application, or for a low-income transportation pass. Send the correct paperwork, filled out beforehand as completely as possible with checkmarks indicating the spaces the doctor must fill out. Give the doctor any needed clarifications in writing.

Permanent Housing. Develop a file of housing possibilities listing the eligibility requirements, type and number of units, the contact person and rental price. Visit the housing and talk to the managers to select appropriate facilities and to pave the way for future contacts. Make use of newspaper ads and become acquainted with the directors of rehab properties. To make an appropriate placements in the selection include safety issues as related to the level of dependence of the person. For example, some people benefit from a building with meals or a 24-hour desk. If the homeless person has a history of housing abuses, honest communication by the worker and the applicant together with the manager avoids past housing problems. Remind the new tenant that their behavior reflects on future placements from your agency. Consistent follow-up and contact with managers resolves problems early on and maintains the reputation of your agency.

Mental Health. Counter the stigma of counseling by normalizing a person's experience: "Anyone who has been through what you have would have depression or tremendous stress. Everyone needs support. It is an opportunity to get over a hump or to live with greater ease." Highlight what might be helpful to share with the counselor in order to get help. As appropriate, offer to accompany the person to the first interview or offer with written permission to share with the counselor any history that may be helpful. This written summary, given ahead of the interview to the counselor about the person's history and your observations can be helpful. Discuss with the homeless person as needed your respect of their confidentiality with the counselor.

continued

Practical Tips to Case Management

Transportation. Flexibility of the worker to give transport to the homeless person expedites services. Trained staff aides or volunteer drivers expand the program's services by assisting people to appointments and participation in programs. Transportation help is especially important for the disabled and seniors.

Time Management. Triage or prioritizing needs is part of work with homeless persons. The demands on the personnel are always greater than the resources. Maintaining the organizational structures, staff support, support services, and advocacy work to eliminate homelessness and planning for future funding are top priorities. Flexibility to deal with emergencies must be built into the program. The bulk of the agency time needs to be guarded for its mission. If the mission is direct services, then the goal is to be as efficient and effective as possible. Periodic evaluation of structure, support services, personnel, and mission effectiveness keeps the wheels rolling smoothly.

SUMMARY

The worker assists the homeless person to rediscover lost goals. Getting in touch with these goals and the desires that drive them rekindles hope and energy. Once the homeless person gets in touch with their personal goals they are prepared to weigh their desires, to look at realistic options, and think of consequences before making a choice.

The worker aids the homeless person to achieve their personal goals. A list of goals of the homeless person are:

1. Immediate Needs
2. Temporary Housing
3. Available Finances
4. Identification and Paperwork
5. Healthcare and Employment or Disability Determination
6. Permanent Housing
7. Special Needs: Counseling

The timing is dependent on the needs and abilities of that person. Creative strategies are a necessary part of overcoming individual and agency obstacles to achieve their goals. Consultation often helps find these hard-to-come-by solutions.

The worker steadies the homeless person's motivation through encouragement, planned one-on-one visits, and inclusion in community activities. This participation in a supportive community affirms their individual capabilities.

Skill-building exercises in which the worker first applies the process of determining goals and desires to their own life, and then the homeless person are included. A section called "Practical Tips to Case Management" addresses in detail how the worker can effectively assist the homeless person to apply for needed resources.

GC by Corrine Lund

CHAPTER 5 *ADVOCATING AND NETWORKING TOGETHER*

Lovie Burkes, who was 63 years old and homeless three years, publicly testified[16] and advocated for the funding needs of homeless senior women. "Staying out on the concrete, was hard on me ... [You fear they are] going to rape you." Lovie through her experience (see Chapter 1) became the expert. Her voice, once raised in terror to scoff away strangers, told of her ignominy. She had once borne her pain in isolation and silence. With support, she gained her own voice. She was able to educate the public about the needs of the homeless senior woman.

Through telling the powerful tragic truth of homelessness, Lovie and others caused the Oakland Commission and Department of Aging to provide housing for homeless seniors and to work for increased affordable housing for the elderly in Oakland.

Lovie's 360-degree turn from isolation and homelessness to self-belief and advocacy depended on others first advocating forcefully on her behalf. It took the united advocacy of a coalition of homeless agencies to overcome the barriers in getting the resources she needed.

THE NEED FOR A TRUSTED ADVOCATE

Lovie had no resources. "I was really in a pickle. I did not have enough money to get back [to relatives in Youngstown, Ohio]." She could not find her family members that used to live in Oakland. She trusted no one.

A senior man named John, who was at risk of homelessness himself because of a lobotomy, became her friend. Lovie recounts the following:

> John saw me and asked me how I was doing. He asked if I wanted a cup of coffee. Every day he came. He said "It's a shame for you to be out here." He took me to breakfast. He said, "Come on and stay with me until you get yourself a place." I was on the couch. We would buy groceries. John liked corn flakes. We got along fine. I love John. He treated me well. He was not like the others.

John depleted his check for extra rent and food for Lovie. Periodically he came to St. Mary's for free groceries. The landlady attempted to reinstate Lovie's SSI (see note 14). Lovie did not trust the landlady. Lovie stated how other problems arose:

> [The landlady] wanted to be my payee (A person who would be in charge of Lovie's finances.) I gave her the wrong Social Security number.
> The landlady did not want me running water. [She said that Lovie ran up a water bill in the thousands of dollars.]
> The landlady told me I was going to have to move. She said, "If John keeps you, I am going to put him out."

Lovie was back outside under the freeway. During this time Lovie became a regular at St. Mary's Drop-in Center. She dropped by the office for a weekly loan against her General Assistance check (GA, see note 3). The loan started at two-dollars. This deepened trust. I broached the topic of my helping her with her finances. The next day she brought her Social Security number. I telephoned the Social Security Office to help Lovie receive her disability. I explained that Lovie was too disabled to call for herself and that she still became very hostile at unpredictable times. I ran into a total impasse. The worker refused to let me speak on Lovie's behalf.

Network With Other Agencies

When I began work with the homeless, my supervisor Carol Cook (the originator of the idea of St. Mary's homeless senior program) directed me to a countywide network of homeless service providers and advocates. It was this network that scheduled a meeting between the service workers and the County Social Services. This exchange acted as a stepping stone. From this meeting, we developed the GA (see note 3) procedure in which disabled seniors' needs could be met even if they could not go into the office.

With these new procedures, I gained access to GA for Lovie. I became the flexible link. I made the system adapt to her. As a result, Lovie, acquired her rightful benefit of GA to pay for minimal housing and food.

Advocacy and Networking for Mental Health Outreach

Lovie's actions still spoke of her inner terror. I contacted an agency for mental health needs of seniors. They said they could send a psychiatrist to the center to assess Lovie's needs and give her a one-time prescription. I asked Lovie "If I am with you, would you be willing to talk to a counselor, who can maybe give you medicine to help you feel better." Lovie agreed. I sat with Lovie so that she could transfer her trust in me to the psychiatrist. Each morning and evening an assigned volunteer in the Drop-in Center reminded Lovie to take her medicine. Slowly her fears lessened.

Lovie participated more and more in community activities. I invited her to my inner-city convent for a party on her birthday. (I learned in time—for the sake of clear boundaries—to develop neutral homelike places for the seniors to feel welcome and safe.) She said: "Yes, if my friend John can come." (John at this time was at times incontinent. I prayed that he didn't have an accident to embarrass himself and make it unpleasant for others.) I said, "O.K." A month later, Lovie attended a Christmas party at the convent. She noticed a TV in the guest room. I think she may have wanted to watch TV. Two days went by and she asked: "Can I stay with you a few days?"

My heart gave a leap! This was my chance to transition her to the inside. But how? I invited her to stay with me at the convent for two days.

The second day she was at the convent, I rented a room for Lovie in a low-income hotel where we assisted seniors to transition from the street. As a ploy to get Lovie comfortable with the room, I asked her to help me set up the room for "someone." This she did willingly.

The next morning, Lovie was sadly leaving, after her two days at the convent were over. As I drove her to the center, I broached my plan with some nervousness. I said, "Lovie, do you remember the room we fixed up in the hotel yesterday. Well, that is your room, if you want it. Here are the keys. You can just put your belongings in it during the day. Or, you can sleep in it."

Lovie, visibly agitated, said, "How will the rent be paid? I will be told to leave." I told her, "Remember you signed a paper saying that I was to help you with your money. You don't have to worry about it. I will pay the rent." Till evening she mulled over the decision. I asked her what she decided. Lovie said, "I'll move in." With great relief, I transported her and her sleeping bag and blankets to the hotel.

Community Volunteers and Interns

To expand our small staff, St. Mary's Center invited community volunteers and applied to be a college training site. In return for the services rendered, the center provided supervision. One of these interns, Jim, and Lovie became fast friends.

Things seemed to proceed pretty well at the hotel for about a month. Lovie was adjusting to having her own place. Then, I received an anxious call from the hotel manager. "The hall in the hotel is badly damaged." He suspected Lovie had let the water run. This report was similar to the water problem when she had stayed with her friend John. I assured the manager that I would discuss this with Lovie. Lovie denied running the water. I asked the manager for time so I could find Lovie a board and care home (see note 9).

Advocacy—Moving Up the Ladder

Lovie really needed the amount of money provided by SSI to afford to move into a board and care home. Because by myself I could not elicit SSI's response to Lovie's need, I moved up the ladder of authority. My supervisor signed a letter to the SSI director that explained my work and Lovie's situation. Shortly afterward, I received a cooperative call from SSI. They let Lovie sign the forms without ever going into the SSI office.

Developing Resources in the Community

I canvassed a number of board and care facilities. Tinnie Winfrey, a director with special training in helping seniors with mental and addiction problems (and a love of challenges), invited Lovie to visit her facility. With great trepidation, Lovie visited the home. She liked Tinnie, but she was still too agitated to move in.

A month later, the manager from the hotel called and said that there was another flood in the hotel and that Lovie must move. Because so many of the tenants in the hotel were from our agency, I pleaded with the hotel manager for a little longer time. Because of her delusions, Lovie was still anxious about a move.

Tinnie and I problem-solved for Lovie to meet with the facility's psychiatrist. After hesitation, Lovie consented. I again accompanied her to aid the transfer of trust. The psychiatrist prescribed a stronger dosage to "help her with her voices." In a few days Lovie was calmer. She let her friend Jim move her to the home. *Finally,* Lovie had a permanent home. Through carefully monitored medicine, Lovie was able to live comfortably without her delusional voices of fear.

One Contact Leads to Another

The psychiatrist from Lovie's board and care became director of St. Luke's Day Program in Oakland for those with mental disorders. Lovie willing attended this program. The staff there reconnected her to her family in Youngstown, Ohio. Lovie explains how this happened:

> At St. Luke's, Candace helped me call. It had been six or seven years since I'd talked to my daughter. Many of [my family] had changed their numbers. The operator said there was a MA Burkes [Mary Ann]. I said, "I bet that is her." We talked for about an hour. That included Candace. "When are you going to come?" said my daughter. She cried.

ADVOCACY TRAINING

The Elements of Advocacy Training include the following:

- Build Self-esteem
- Provide Background Information
- Model Self Advocacy (by formerly homeless trainers)
- Instruct on Presentation
- Practice With Affirming Feedback
- Rally Group Enthusiasm

Lovie and 11 other seniors spent two days in a beautiful Los Gatos retreat, learning advocacy training. Taking a group to a beautiful retreat setting in itself acknowledged that the participants' gifts were valued.

Uprooting the stigma of being homeless and placing the problem in the systemic policies of the government and society was very important. Through fact-sharing, the participants became aware that robbery of the national low-income housing and human services monies for transfer to military aggressions outside the US borders threw new light on the causes of homelessness. Once they were enlightened that system policies cause homelessness, not their personal failures, their self-esteem was renewed. Then their voices were released, and they could tell of the ignominy of their homeless experience. They felt empowered to advocate for the return of these funds to benefit the basic needs of the poor.

Hearing someone tell their story with clarity and dignity modeled to others how to unmask their experience to educate the public. To practice sharing previously hidden pain in the safety of supportive groups is empowering.

A self-advocacy presentation 1) pinpoints the topic, 2) is brief, and 3) includes the personal story of homelessness. Role playing in front of the group with supportive and corrective feedback builds skill and confidence. A pep rally finale sends all off with zeal.

Advocacy Through Art

A grant from the Cultural Arts Division of the City of Oakland afforded 30 formerly homeless seniors a special opportunity to advocate through art. Their art focused on educating the public about the need to end homelessness. It was displayed in an art exhibition, as a bus bench ad, and a billboard ad. In an accompanying reception, the mayor and state officials shared a platform with the formerly homeless and learned through them that there were many homeless seniors in the city and state (see Chapter 6, Empowerment through Art).

Photo by Carol Younger\The Montclarion

Advocacy, the Media, and Public Officials

The art exhibition brought the seniors into the media. It gave them opportunities to share their stories with reporters. St. Mary's staff and seniors invited a state legislator and greatly increased her awareness that homelessness included seniors.

Practical Tips To Advocacy

Learn the agencies and join with the networks in your locale that also assist homeless persons. Use time before and after meetings to make important contacts with workers from other agencies. Visit other agencies to increase the effectiveness of referrals and joint services. Reach out for information and assistance from other programs. Ask for other leads. Become active in groups to jointly advocate for the needs of the people you serve.

Attempt to remain respectful while advocating because at this time all social services are overwhelmed. If you need to move up the ladder to meet the needs, your approach can be softened. "I know you are doing all you can on your level to assist me. I am wondering if your supervisor can help us move this forward." All connections must be saved because in the future some homeless person will need them. Sometimes I have had to apologize for my impatience.

If Social Security or VA do not provide the rightful government benefits of the person, contact the local office of your congressperson.

Maintain integrity and, therefore, credibility in your interagency dealings.

Develop contacts and be *readily* available to the newspaper or media. They are excellent avenues to educate the public and to provide special advocacy.

The squeaky wheel gets the oil. Be tenacious!

Build in ways to teach and make advocacy training an essential part of your program for staff and homeless persons. In a country such as the US with representative government, advocacy is a basic life skill.

If basic services are not available, for example, prescription drug detoxification for a low-income person, let the local drug and alcohol government agency know of the need.

Plan with the homeless how to invite legislative and local dignitaries, and media to your facilities. Role play before visits to improve skills and confidence.

Provide for a retreat away for homeless persons and staff. A retreat affirms, allows concentrated skill-building, and builds group solidarity.

SKILL BUILDING—Advocacy

- ✓ When you feel strongly about the current issue on homelessness in your area, write a brief letter to the editor of the newspaper.
- ✓ Again, when the spirit strikes you, call your local political officials to inform them of your opinion on this issue. It only takes a minute.
- ✓ Join or create a coalition of advocates working on homeless issues. Plan a strategy with which you could inform local people of influence about the needs of homeless persons.
- ✓ Write a brief outline on what you would say in three minutes to ask your city council for funds for your program for homeless persons.
- ✓ What are ways—small and large—the homeless persons you work with could advocate for themselves? Facilitate a group to assist them in writing a letter or a petition to government officials to express their concerns.

SUMMARY

Advocacy by the homeless worker is the art of becoming the amorphous glue between the homeless person and the rightfully needed services. A supportive network of agencies best breaks the foray of accessibility barriers.

To teach homeless persons the objective economic roots of homelessness lifts their debilitating shame. This frees brave homeless persons to claim the power of their incredible story. Advocacy training, retreats, and art workshops revolutionize the meek. The media catapults them into the public consciousness. Ways to incorporate advocacy and expand networking are varied and can be creatively developed.

CHAPTER 6 *INVITING THE HOMELESS PERSON INTO AN EMPOWERING COMMUNITY*

Community—Poem

Circle of love,
Community.
Come in. Welcome!
You belong.
You are one of us,
  no different.
We accept you.
Come in. Welcome!
Tell us your name.
Please come in.
Do not be afraid.
We care here.
We will give you a cup of coffee.
And we will smile
  as we hand it to you.
We want you here. Yes, you!
Please do not go away.
We belong together. Yes, we do!
We want to laugh at your jokes.
We want to be still with you
  when you share your pain.
We want you clothed and sheltered.
And at our table
  we want you fed to full with nourishing food.
And around this table
  we want you to taste the commingling of us all;
  brown, black, native, Asian, and light,
  the delight we are to each other.
Taste the spicincss, the tart,
  the sweetness, the tang,
  the subtle, the muchness.
And here you belong.
Wc wclcome you. We care about you.

Come join us. Give us your flavor.
It is unique.
Come rest and be strengthened.
Be at home, my friend.
Communion.

FROM HOMELESSNESS TO COMMUNITY

Loneliness and isolation are part and parcel of the downward spiral into homelessness. At times the homeless person's condition, such as an addiction or another mental disorder, limits the person's ability to communicate and keep contact. Often, the agencies designed to assist the needy are cut out or cut back. Then the person falls out of the system. Reentry requires crossing gigantic barriers constructed to limit access because funds are insufficient. Therefore, the homeless person becomes more and more alienated. The person's inability to keep up their appearance causes personal shame and withdrawal. The society likewise withdraws from the specter of its own callousness, unable and unwilling to look the person in the eye. The homeless person becomes the modern leper. And society becomes the uneasy medieval keeper of the stigma. Finally, the vulnerable person isolates themselves for protection against the jungle of the street. The end result of this mutual distancing creates for the homeless person what J, a coworker who was on the streets for three years, calls "a dal'gone lonely world out there."

The following experience I had at St. Mary's exemplifies the emotional isolation of the homeless:

> A tall, attractively groomed 67-year-old woman without any financial resources, wandered around department stores during the day for three years. She was a fiercely proud and private person whose fear did not allow her to answer the questions of those who attempted to assist her. She said, "It is hard day-after-day to look like you're shopping." She added emphatically, "I would rather die than have my family know that I was homeless." The shame of those days was so damning to her personal image that, after she was housed, she emotionally distanced herself from that experience by condemning the "lazy *young* homeless." She never told her family about her experiences.

The sense of community alleviates the loneliness. Persons who come from the street to St. Mary's Center find friendly people who learn their names. At St. Mary's they can chat with someone about the daily events of their lives. They have an opportunity to communicate again. They know that the others also experienced homelessness so they feel accepted and understood, which helps break the power of the shame.

The experience of community reverses society's withdrawal and mends the path back to oneness with the human family. This process of reconnecting starts in the safety of a special, empowering community. In this supportive environment, the person reconnects with a stable life pattern, with a real sense of self, and with personal talents. With a group, the person feels empowered to take actions, such as participating in a rally that affects their own future. In time, with this firm base, they link with family and church.

I always knew when the formerly homeless person was far along in their stabilization because they began to reach out to their family. This means that they can face the questions from their family about their homelessness and that they feel satisfied with their life now. For example, three months after GC (see GC's Story, Chapter 1) had a roof over his head, he felt better about himself. He invited his teenage son for a visit. A few months later, GC enthusiastically reconnected with another son. They started to go fishing together.

How To Build a Community

Many homeless programs build a strong community, or they would not be successful. A variety of approaches to community building can work. To give an example of one way to build a community for the homeless, I will review the steps that took place for the homeless seniors at St. Mary's to show how they evolved into a community. As you will see, the goal of better achieving the seniors' needs sets the pattern for the evolution.

First, I need to say that when I came to St. Mary's Center, there already was a community of workers who saw themselves connected to the broader city community. They served and empowered this broader community. When, as the sole homeless worker, I brought the first seniors into the Center, the other program workers welcomed the seniors and made them feel at home.

As the number of seniors who had their own housing increased, there were too many people for me to see in follow-up visits. I decided it was more practical to gather the seniors together once a week. We started a weekly support meeting. Besides allowing for needed follow-up, the meeting offered an opportunity for me to see how they were doing. Also, if any problems had arisen for them, they could ask for assistance.

Support Groups

The support meetings had a very simple format. First, everyone was welcomed. Then, a topic that flowed from practical life needs was introduced by the leader. For example, the goal might be to help people gain courage to deal with life difficulties. The leader introduced the topic, "How did I manage to deal successfully with a crisis in my life?" and modeled a response by disclosing a personal experience. The leader then suggested other ways to approach the question to jog people's memories and interest. The leader invited each person to begin by introducing themselves by name and encouraged everyone to say at least a few words on the topic. The leader provided an atmosphere where each person could share to the degree they felt comfortable. Through modeling and directives, the leader asked the participants to listen in a supportive way to each other. New people received a special welcome and a chance to share a little about themselves. The meeting ended with announcements, and people were encouraged to affirm each other for coming to make their group worthwhile for each other. All were invited to the meal that followed in the main dining room. The support meeting was scheduled so that it would precede the meal. The meal served as a big drawing card.

At different times in the year, the format of the support meeting changed. Around election time, a video explaining ballot issues was shown. The goal was to present stimulating and relevant topics. As one senior said, "It gives you something to think about instead of being down all the time." The support group empowered people to speak their own thoughts and to listen to others—the art of communication. The process of resocialization took place together.

The development of a group for the homeless takes much effort and persistence. It is an uphill process. I reminded and encouraged people to come. I provided transportation for those who physically or psychologically could not make it on their own. When people did not come, I let them know they were missed. It took months before the group size increased and became stable. Developing a group for the homeless is not easy. I feel that any good community development takes consistent and continuing effort. If efforts are not made to aid a group's growth, the group will die. For community development of homeless persons, this is doubly true.

A Drop-in Center

The support group at St. Mary's gave impetus to the idea of starting a Drop-in Center where the seniors could come daily. After getting the space for a Drop-in Center, we raised the monies for staff. We received a young Holy Cross Associate[17] who for a stipend spent ten months a year with St. Mary's. Because the Holy Cross Volunteer Program is also built on the community model, the female volunteer brought that perspective. With her youthfulness, she also brought enthusiasm. She listened to the stories of the seniors which opened up a whole new world to her. It was very affirming to the seniors.

When the seniors realized the Drop-in Center was set aside as their own place, the community formation jumped strongly forward. It became a place where new seniors were welcomed, and they, in turn, learned to welcome others. The Drop-in Center became a "home."

After the initial interview when a new homeless person came to the office, often, I led the person out to the Drop-in Center. I introduced them to someone "who had been there." I prompted the conversation along certain lines so that the homeless person could see before their eyes what they, too, could achieve. Then I left them, so they could form a bond.

People came to the Drop-in Center every day. Some said it was like their rehab place because they hung around there instead of Old Man's Park known for its drugs. At the Drop-in Center, they played cards, shot the breeze, and listened to music.

In retrospect, the community formation could probably have started faster, if it had begun with the Drop-in Center instead of the support groups. But, the deeper community development came from the quality of sharing in the support groups.

During the annual evaluation of the homeless program, the community aspect always receives the most positive feedback from the seniors. It is always the "friendly people," "the sharing," and "new friends," that are most strongly valued.

Community Is Healing

Community building is not an icing on the cake of a homeless program; it is an essential part. Community is where the healing takes place. Someone might come who was angry, manipulative, and distrustful, but slowly a transformation took place. The person came out of their shell; they offered their own ideas, and they laughed. They interacted, and offered to pour a cup of coffee for another. The walls came down; the self-esteem increased, and friendships were built.

A sense of belonging is an important part of the healing. The basic needs of housing, food, and clothing are primary. But, so are a person's social needs. It is in the relating that a person feels part of something that is going to last for at least some time. Personal friendships do not have to end. The sense of security helps the self to stabilize. The Drop-in Center is a safe environment to relearn skills of communication and other skills. People are with those who are going through the same experience of dusting themselves off from a fall or near-fall to the streets. Here—with their community—their experience is respected and treated openly. This, too, is healing.

Sense of the Broader Community

The empowering art work mentioned in the previous chapter and displayed in these pages continued each year at St. Mary's. By the fourth year, the seniors reached out to the fourth graders of a neighboring school. Together they did collages about themselves on outlines of their bodies. The elders and fourth graders sang, drew, exchanged stories, and described their art to each other.

MH, one of the seniors, explained, "I had these powerful feelings when at the third or fourth art session with the children. I felt like we all belonged together. We are all human beings."

A sense of being connected to the broader community keeps a group stretching and watching out for their own interests, as well as contributing to the broader community. It is necessary for the maturity of a group. The seniors grew to feel that they had a mission to educate the public.

EMPOWERMENT

To empower means the worker recognizes the gifts of the person and assists them to develop these gifts. The worker notices the talents and interests during the initial interview and during follow-up contacts. The worker encourages the person who can write letters, lead meetings, read poetry, share creative ideas, and lead AA (Alcohol Anonymous) meetings to use these gifts for the group. The worker provides education and support for the person. As the group benefits from the homeless person's talents, at the same time, the person rebuilds their own sense of self-worth.

To teach new skills is a balancing act: to get far enough back for a person to experience their own strength and yet close enough to support them.

Education and training for self-advocacy in Chapter 5 are essentially empowerment. Using a retreat for a training opportunity was also an important factor. That was one experience of empowerment that I will never forget.

Empowerment Starts With the Workers

The workers themselves must function as a mutually empowering community that supports the gifts and initiative of each member. Then, this style is passed on to the people that are served.

Empowerment of workers includes the following:

- Clarifying the Shared Mission
- Supporting Each Member
- Envisioning Oneself As a Team
- Providing Ongoing Training
- Calling Forth Each Member's Gifts
- Communicating Consistently
- Incorporating Ideas of Staff Into the Program
- Evaluating Annually Together All Aspects of the Program.

Empowering Through Participation to Leadership

To develop a peer leadership group, the homeless group is taught to conduct a meeting with a clear format. The worker's role is simply to assist the group to learn how to empower each other as peers. The peers encourage one another to get involved, make decisions, and bring ideas to the larger group. Developing a peer leadership board is a learning process that takes time. The process will have many spurts and even false starts. Leadership is fostered by training and encouragement.

A group like a peer board needs to know the extent of its authority. When their authority is respected, it encourages the group. On the other hand, to act as if the group has power, but to really keep all the power as a director or staff is very disempowering. Also, to give a group authority and then to dissolve the group or its authority disillusions its members.

As an example of how empowerment continues to develop in a program, I again use an experience from St. Mary's. The seniors learned from the Holy Cross Associate how to welcome new seniors and to manage the Drop-in Center. Over the course of two years, leadership among the seniors developed. One of the seniors, with the help of others, took on the responsibility of the Drop-in Center. The seniors took ownership. They were proud of their room and their management of it.

In the support group I often said, "This is *your* group. Thank each other for coming." And "This is your picnic. What do *you* want to eat? How are *you* going to pay for it?" And "This is *your* Christmas party. When and where do you want to have it?" I worked at having the perspective "not mine, but *yours*." The sense of ownership of the program motivated people to give themselves to its future.

Doing for rather than preparing a group *to do* a project themselves militates against empowerment. For example, sometimes a well-meaning person chooses to give a group a picnic, rather than provide money for a group to make their own choices. If the group gives itself the picnic, they congratulate themselves on what they accomplished for the group. And the next year, if they want something changed, they remember to change it. So during the annual picnic of St. Mary's, those seniors who now had resources gave enough for those who still did not have their lives stabilized. The seniors who did the grilling set up early and took pride in their work. By the sixth year, it was like clockwork with four people each at one grill. They were efficient and proud of themselves. The group was appreciative of their efforts. On the other hand, if a group only receives, this breaks down the group. Soon, each person is trying to manipulate to get the most. People start complaining because things are being done *to them* rather than *their doing* things.

An empowering philosophy asks the question, "Are the participants making more and more of the decisions and carrying out more and more of the leadership?"

Empowerment Through Art

Throughout this book the reader sees art produced by formerly homeless seniors. This unbelievably empowering experience began when the artist Roxanne Hills dreamed up the idea to get a grant from the City of Oakland Cultural Arts Division for the seniors and her to work together (see Chapter 5). The art educated the public. The staff that knew the seniors thought they would like the idea, so the artist and staff thoroughly introduced it. The seniors were open to the idea and, in time, developed enthusiasm for the project. Most of them had not done art since they were in grade school. An important part of the grant was recognizing that the work of the seniors was important. They were given a stipend of $10 for each session they participated in if they completed all eight sessions. This was effective motivation. First Roxanne led them in drawing self-portraits (see the book cover) which was very empowering. She taught them how to appreciate the strength of their own work. Their uncertain strokes soon developed into enthusiastic dabbing of paint.

During the project, the homeless senior painters encouraged each other. A sense of comradeship grew, and the atmosphere of the gathering took on its own life. Developing the creative part of themselves while turning their experience of homelessness from a stigma into advocacy was a healing experience. By the eighth session, when each was drawing the possible billboard ad, you could have heard a pin drop. The energy in the room was everyone's stretching together to accomplish a goal. It was an energy of new life, a healing energy. (The drawing that was placed on the billboard is on page 88.)

One Empowerment Leads to Another

One day in the later stages of writing this book, I talked with GC. He had recently discovered the whereabouts of his fifth child and was planning an out-of-state visit to him. Daily he was drawing sketches—a life-long love that began again as soon as he had a roof over his head. He was willing to continue to colead training sessions for workers who help the homeless and to participate in the distribution of this book. He even hoped to coordinate the homeless seniors around painting boxes for a small fund-raising project. I was delighted that he felt confident enough to share his knowledge and talents for himself and others. I realized how far GC had advanced in the last two and a half years, since we met him at the marina.

SKILL BUILDING—Empowering in community

The following are best shared in a staff discussion group:

✓ List your personal community connections and write next to each what that connection does to empower your life.

✓ Discuss and list the ways in your contacts with homeless persons how you and your agency can empower them to build community?

✓ Remember an experience where someone recognized your gifts and facilitated their development. What were the elements of the process that made it successful? How can you apply that process to your work?

✓ How does the management style and the staff meetings of your agency empower you as a team, so you are able to share that style of empowerment with homeless persons? How can the agency empowerment be improved?

✓ Tell practical ways of sharing life skills and using encouragement, so that you empower homeless persons to do things for themselves. Try a situation such as discerning when, and to what degree, you assist someone in a phone call. Discuss the principle of being close enough to teach and be a support, yet far back enough to give people the opportunity to test their own strength and build their confidence.

✓ What way does your program develop the talents of the people you assist so as to bring them into ownership and leadership in your program? Is it clear what decisions or effect on decision-making the program participants have?

SUMMARY

Loneliness and isolation are part and parcel of the downward spiral into homelessness. The sense of community alleviates the loneliness. The experience of community reverses society's withdrawal and mends the path back to oneness with the human family. This process of reconnecting starts in the safety of a special, empowering community.

Building a strong community is an essential of a successful homeless program. Many approaches to community building are effective. The steps of evolution will be dictated by the needs of that group. For example, the St. Mary's Homeless Senior Program developed support groups first to be able to keep in touch with a large number of people who were already housed but had follow-up needs. From these support groups, a Drop-in Center developed.

Community building is not an icing on the cake of a homeless program but essential. Community is where the healing takes place. A sense of belonging is an important part of the healing. To relearn communication in a safe environment with others who were homeless is also healing.

A sense of being connected to the broader community keeps a group stretching and watching out for their own interests, as well as contributing to the broader community. It is necessary for the maturity of a group.

To empower means the worker recognizes the gifts of the homeless person and assists them to develop these gifts. To teach new skills is a balancing act: to get far enough back for a person to experience their own strength and yet close enough to support them.

Empowerment starts with the workers. The workers themselves must function as a mutually empowering community that supports the gifts and initiative of each member. This style is then passed on to the people that are served.

Peer leadership is fostered by training and encouragement. To develop a peer-leadership group, the homeless group is taught to conduct a meeting with a clear format. The worker's role is simply to assist the group to learn how to empower each other. The sense of ownership of the program motivates people to give themselves to its future. One of the things that diminish empowerment is doing for a group what they could manage to do for themselves.

Throughout this book, the reader sees art produced by the formerly homeless seniors. This was an unbelievably empowering experience. One empowerment leads to another.

Skill-building exercises in which the worker reflects on aspects of the power of community and on how to effectively empower the homeless are also included.

I WisHED I WAS OUT OF ThE CoLd

CHAPTER 7 *SUSTAINING THE MOTIVATION OF THE WORKER*

The Spirit Leads in the Dance—Poem

The spirit leads in the dance.
The spirit gives the life.
The spirit leads in the dance.
Get with the spirit.
Feel the rhythm.
Move in beat.
Inward, listen.
Do you hear?
  Follow.
  Follow.
Relax. Trust it all.
The spirit leads in the dance.
  Follow.
  Follow.
Hear the rhythm?
Dance the beat.
  Follow.
  Follow.
Oh, the joy of it all!

THE STRESSES OF WORKING WITH THE HOMELESS

Workers who assist homeless people experience great stress. They will encounter deep pain in the homeless person. It is part of the worker's job to try to help the homeless person alleviate difficulties that exist in layers untouched over the years. And finally, there is the task of advocating with the homeless to government agencies that provide extremely limited resources and are often unresponsive. Each of these challenges is difficult and takes much energy.

WAYS TO MAINTAIN THE WORKER'S MOTIVATION

The importance of the worker's motivation is touched on in this book's Introduction. Each worker must truly desire to work with the homeless. This desire which goes far beyond the necessary paycheck is the wellspring of an individual worker's motivation. This wellspring must be guarded and nourished.

Chapter 6 explains the importance of building a supportive community among the workers of community and the process for doing this. Another dynamic that sustains the worker's motivation is a sense that someone or something bigger than oneself is in charge of this mission. This belief that there is a Higher Power that has the wisdom, strength, and love to direct the project, allows the worker to draw from this Source. With this assurance, the workers can realize they are not alone and need not feel overburdened with the task.

Focus on the mission keeps all the workers looking in the same direction. It cuts down on the distractions from interpersonal friction, competitions, and insecurities. This focus is maintained by the team's setting goals together, selecting objectives to achieve these goals, and frequently restating the goals at weekly meetings, in supervision, and at special events. A yearly review of the goals, and evaluation of the organizational programs in light of the goals is a must. If goals and objectives of a program are clear to each worker, then everyone can pull together.

When the special spirit that each worker adds to the program is appreciated, this forms a strong basis for good communication and cooperation. When each worker feels acknowledged as an important member of the team, this encourages and supports the worker.

THE PRACTICE OF CENTERING

A practice of starting each meeting with a few minutes of centering helps ground the group. Hints of ways to center might be shared, including the following:

- sitting straight with feet on the floor,
- being aware of one's body and relaxing the parts that have tension,
- breathing deeply,
- clearing one's mind,
- entering in one's mind to a quiet, safe place of peace.

Centering can be initiated creatively with a reflective opening, such as a reading or a song. The centering can be done while holding hands which reminds the workers they are a community.

Centering allows the worker to get in touch with their own Inner Source. It is a means of dipping into the wellspring that provides the energy, love, and wisdom for the mission. This centering allows the worker to relax into that listening space to be in touch with that greater strength. It reminds the worker that they are not alone in the endeavor and that "The Spirit Leads in the Dance."

PRESERVING THE WORKER'S ENERGY

The worker's energy is preserved by matching well the person with the tasks for which they are best suited. The majority of tasks that a worker does each day must be something they enjoy doing. This needs to be formalized in a clear job description.

Support of the worker includes scheduled staff meetings and regular longer meetings that provide training. Individual or group supervision is very helpful. Clear communication and planning of varying tasks is necessary.

The skills necessary to be successful are often so great the inexperienced worker can at times be discouraged. There is a danger that the worker—in self-defense—might blame the homeless person. This discouragement can be avoided by providing consistent support, education, and supervision for new workers.

Affirmation of the worker by acknowledging the challenging nature of the work and its grave importance is basic. Opportunities for workers to acknowledge talents, accomplishments, and important events in each other's lives need to be included to create a positive environment.

Encouraging the individual worker to take time to renew themselves is essential. After three years of work with the homeless, I took a leave for one month for a quiet retreat for myself. The retreat was like an oasis. I came back ready to dive in for another three years. Employee policies need to allow this flexibility, so that the worker can enjoy respites such as a retreat. Then, the individual will have the energy for this draining work.

DEVELOPING RELATIONSHIPS WITH PROPER BOUNDARIES

The worker who is drawn to care for the needs of the homeless is often a caregiver in their own families. To know how to be a caregiver in a balanced way is an art. The key to this art is forming the right type of relationship with the homeless person. The most common pitfall for a natural caregiver is over-identification or codependency. The topic of codependency is addressed in many excellent self-help books. The pitfalls can be avoided by taking pointers from these books and discussing them one at a time at the beginning of a staff meeting, or to have periodic mini-trainings. Other important resources are the 12-step Codependency Groups and other similar education-support groups.

Three Types of Relationship

The type of relationship between the worker and the homeless person determines the effectiveness in assisting the homeless person and empowering them to remain stable. This also determines greatly the amount of stress that the worker might carry home from work.

There are three types of relationships:

- Empathetic
- Over-Identified
- Sympathetic[18]

Empathetic

A relationship that has quality and proper distance is paramount. The optimal relationship between the worker and homeless person is an empathetic relationship. The quality of an empathetic relationship is built on the worker's understanding in a visceral way the situation of the homeless person. The worker is very open and responsive to the needs of the homeless person while at the same time remaining well centered. The worker forms a caring bond yet keeps enough distance to stay objective. I often call this "walking in someone else's shoes, but at the same time realizing that they are not your shoes."

An example of an empathetic relationship is the following:

> Mary was a 65-year-old woman who was living with a friend and needed to move on or the friend would lose her lease. Mary felt great pressure. On top of this, Mary had delusions of a religious nature that caused her discomfort. Mary was somewhat paranoid and had avoided seeing a doctor for years. The worker respected Mary's fears and listened openly as she shared her feelings. The worker made sincere reflective comments, such as, "That must be very uncomfortable," or "This caused a lot of pressure in

your life." The facial and postural expression of the worker let Mary know the worker regretted that she was going through these difficulties.

The diagram that follows represents the empathetic relationship: two circles facing each other with communication flowing back and forth. The worker and the homeless person each have two consciousnesses: one of self and one of the other during this exchange. In this exercise, the worker needs to be aware of these interconnected consciousnesses and their meaning on themselves and the homeless person.

The worker needs to analyze how they see self as well as the other (the homeless person). The worker needs to also be aware of how the homeless person possibly sees self and other (the worker). For example, in the empathetic relationship, the worker sees self as supportive and encouraging and the homeless person as capable and in pain. The worker images that the homeless person sees self as capable and yet being cared for at this time and sees the worker as understanding and respectful.

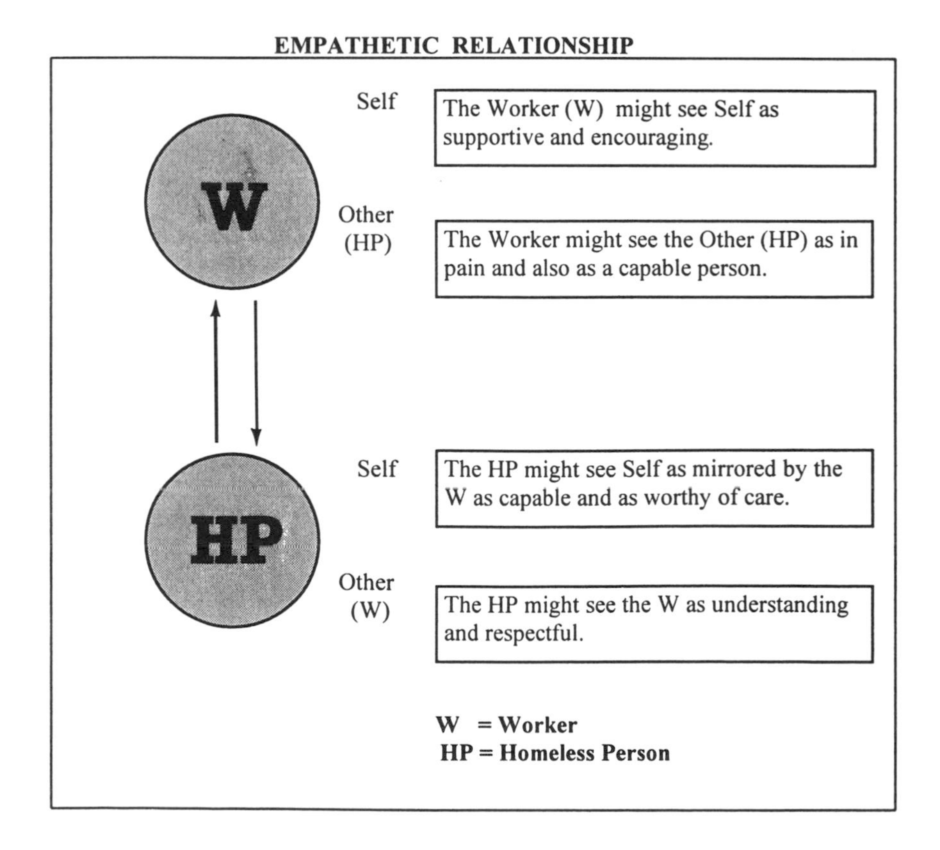

The worker in this relationship keeps the problem and the responsibility with the homeless person. The worker might empathetically suffer some, especially if the system is imposing unbearable demands on people with very limited capabilities. But the worker keeps centered and does not take this as a personal problem. This moderates the stress the worker takes home.

Over-identified Relationship

In an over-identified relationship, the worker loses a sense of objectivity with the homeless person. The worker is assuming the circumstances of the person coming for help are the same as a personal past experience. The following is an example:

> A couple was referred from a shelter to St. Mary's Center for help with housing. The shelter staff reported that in their two nights with them they saw no signs of addictions in the couple. At St. Mary's the interview was very brief, and the couple talked about losing housing because the landlord was unreasonable. The worker did not verify this. The worker moved quickly to see what the couple's needs were for housing. It was Christmas time, and the worker had a personal goal of placing the couple before Christmas. This meant that the Center had lent both the deposit and the first month's rent. The worker quickly arranged for transportation of the couple's belongings. The worker offered the couple food and the loan of a toaster and TV without their asking for them. When the first of the month came, the couple did not pay the loan as promised and were using alcohol. The wife ended up in the hospital after being badly beaten up by the husband.

The over-identified relationship is illustrated in the diagram below by the circles representing the worker and homeless person overlapping to demonstrate the merging of boundaries that is taking place. The worker in this case sees self as capable and caring and the homeless person as needy and helpless. In this case, the homeless person sees self as able to manipulate and the worker as someone that can be conned.

The worker becomes very stressed in this situation. There is emotional confusion and the worker relives past unresolved conflicts. The worker might emotionally or literally take the person home. A warning sign that this type of relationship is taking place is preoccupation on off-hours with the homeless person's problems. Losing sleep is also a sign that the worker has crossed the boundary.

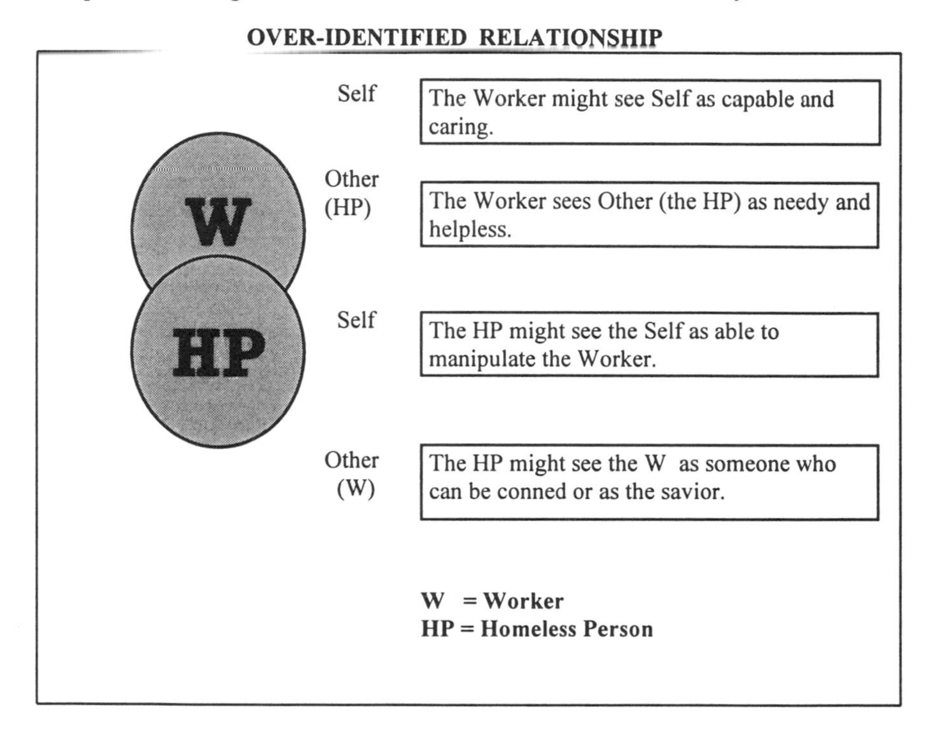

Sympathetic Relationship

In a sympathetic relationship, the worker knows the homeless person has some needs but does not allow themselves to really care what happens to the homeless person. The worker may feel some pity but keeps themselves aloof from forming any real bond. For example, if a worker is tired and does not want to deal with another homeless person before leaving for the day, the worker might say, "I am sorry but you will have to come back tomorrow when I am free." There is no real eye contact or desire to understand the real situation.

The sympathetic relationship is represented in the diagram below by two circles that are distant. The communication is fragmented so broken lines are drawn between the worker and the homeless person. In this case, the worker sees self as unavailable and the homeless person as intrusive. The homeless person probably sees self as not important and the worker as uncaring and unresponsive.

In the sympathetic relationship, the worker does not even see the shoes of the homeless person. The worker does not allow themselves to be close enough to listen and discover the real difficulties of the person. The worker makes no attempt to imagine what it would be like to walk in the shoes of the homeless person.

SYMPATHETIC RELATIONSHIP

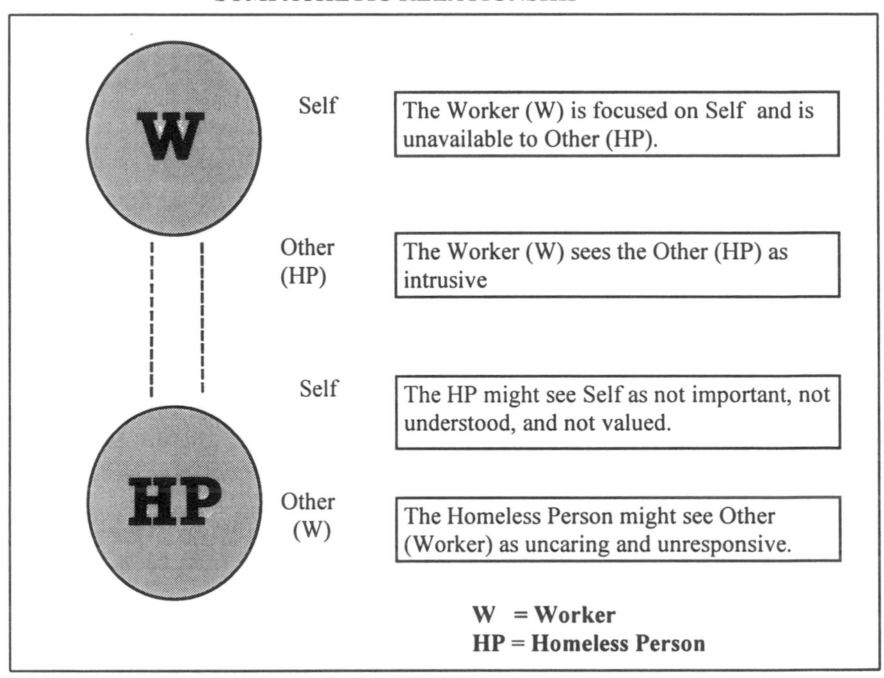

In the sympathetic relationship, the worker might feel the stress of being ineffective and unsatisfied in their work. Even if the worker does not realize this, the supervisor soon will. The sympathetic relationship may be the result of a lack of understanding of the homeless person's experience, personal prejudices, a lack of desire to do this work, a lack of relational skills, or being burnt out. A worker may start out mainly with an empathetic or over-identified relationship and move toward a sympathetic relationship. A worker who tends to form over-identified relationships may become overwhelmed by the feelings and the work. They may become disappointed or burnt-out. The worker might then begin to want to distance themselves from the homeless person to protect themselves. This worker needs to understand their own over-identification and work on new ways of relating. The worker who ordinarily forms empathetic relationships must realize that this type of relating takes energy and needs to pace themselves. If the empathetic worker sees themselves slipping into a sympathetic relationship by withdrawing from relationships, this is a warning sign to find ways to replenish and conserve energy.

SKILL BUILDING—Developing an empathetic relationship

✓ In the center of a group (fishbowl), two people role play an interaction between a worker and a homeless person. After the interaction the role players first make use of the above diagrams to select the type of relationship—empathetic, over-identified or sympathetic—and how they saw self and the other during the sharing. Observers describe the interaction as one of the three types or parts of one of the three types and explain why. Then they add their perceptions to the diagram of self and other.

✓ Divide into groups of two and take turns role playing a work situation. After the role play, discuss how the worker and the homeless person each saw self and the other. Decide which of the three types of the relationship it most resembled.

✓ Because all workers have all three types of relationships at times, think of a time when you formed each type of relationship. Fill in the boxes of the corresponding diagram as fully as possible for that interaction. Discuss these as a group.

SKILL BUILDING—Review of relationship and housing

✓ The type of relationship will affect how the worker will relate and respond to the homeless person in each step. To review the overall material of this book in light of the type of relationship, *complete* the chart that follows as a group. Consider how the type of the relationship will affect each step of working with a homeless person. There are many different possible responses.

For example, in the empathetic relationship when the worker reaches out to the homeless person in a pace that matches that of the homeless person this creates a space for the homeless person to feel safe. In an over-identified relationship, the worker rushes ahead with their own agenda. The homeless person may feel dependent or fearful. In a sympathetic relationship, the worker will be so distant, inconsistent, and nonsupportive that the homeless person may feel fearful and will likely not come inside.

EMPATHETIC RELATIONSHIP

Steps	The Worker	The Homeless Person
Reaches out	Matches pace	Feels safe
Builds trust	Slowly and steadily	Knows what to expect
Understands	Objective	Feels comfortable sharing
Works toward goals		
Advocates/networks		
Empowers		

OVER-IDENTIFIED RELATIONSHIP

Steps	The Worker	The Homeless Person
Reaches out	Rushes ahead with own agenda	Feels fearful or dependent
Builds trust	Creates dependency	Expects lots of help
Understands	Subjective	Feels confused
Works toward goals		
Advocates/networks		
Empowers		

SYMPATHETIC RELATIONSHIP

Steps	The Worker	The Homeless Person
Reaches out	Responds too slowly to needs	Feels fearful
Builds trust	Does not trust	Does not trust
Understands	Subjective	Feels not understood
Works toward goals		
Advocates/networks		
Empowers		

SUMMARY

The worker who assists homeless people experiences great stress because they encounter deep pain in the homeless person and difficulties that exist in layers untouched over the years. Government agencies are often unresponsive.

The worker's motivation must be maintained. Ways to sustain this motivation include the following:

- Guard and sustain the worker's desire to assist the homeless.
- Share the belief that there is a Higher Power whose wisdom, strength, and love direct and sustain the mission through centering.
- Keep the focus on the mission.
- Match well the person with the task for which they are best suited.
- Support the worker by supervision, meetings, communication, planning, training, and validation of their work.
- Provide flexible work schedules so workers can have periods of personal renewal.

A major way the worker maintains energy is developing relationships with proper boundaries. The key is the art of forming the right type of relationship with the homeless person. There are three types of relationship:

> *empathetic*—The worker is very open and responsive to the needs of the homeless person while at the same time they keep enough distance to be objective.
> *over-identified*—The worker is assuming that the circumstances of the person coming for help are the same as a personal past experience.
> *sympathetic*—The worker feels some pity for the homeless person but keeps a distance so no real relationship is formed.

The empathetic relationship best maintains the worker's energy and empowers the homeless person. A worker may start out mainly with an empathetic or an over-identified relationship but with burnout may move toward a sympathetic relationship. Diagrams and exercises are included.

CHAPTER 8 *HOMELESS SENIORS*

EXPERIENCES OF SENIORS ON THE STREET

J:	Shelters? I never went to them. They are unsafe. People always robbed you in shelters. I slept in abandoned cars, parks. It was safer.
Lovie:	I used to sleep [under the freeway] on 6th. But I started getting company. I moved.
Charlie:	I had health problems. I just thought it was old age. I had arthritis. I had two walking sticks. [And I had] glaucoma. With [my drinking] alcohol, I didn't know how serious it was.
William:	If you are in a shelter, you have to get up at five [a.m.] and [are] not in until ten [p.m.]. [So] you are out on the streets all the time. You have no place to rest.

SPECIAL DIFFICULTIES OF HOMELESS SENIORS

Vulnerability

The number one difficulty of seniors[19] out on the street is their physical vulnerability. "It is a jungle out there," said William, who was seventy and dragged one leg in his tottering walk. Homeless seniors realize that they cannot protect themselves by fending off others or by running.

Their physical vulnerability causes seniors to shy away from shelters. In the shelters they fear they will be assaulted or robbed, so homeless seniors usually find an out-of-the-way place protected from the elements. It is their "home," where they can go each night. It might be an abandoned car or a sheltered doorway. Because few seniors go to shelters, the number of homeless seniors is under reported.

The City of Seattle addresses the vulnerability of homeless seniors by providing a shelter that is just for those 55 and older. When seniors are with homeless people their own age, they feel less fearful.

At St. Mary's Center we considered safety a key factor for seniors. We found that seniors were more willing to come off the street if we placed them in relatively safe hotel rooms rather than in shelters.

Health Issues

Healthcare issues increase with the aging process. Homelessness militates against proper healthcare. The homeless person finds it difficult to obtain proper and nutritious food. In most urban communities there are usually resources that prevent starvation. But a homeless person cannot control the type of food they eat or its quality. The homeless senior with a lack of funds is unable to meet special dietary needs necessary for health.

To stay alive many homeless persons have to worry about food, the elements, and avoiding danger. Regular attention to healthcare goes by the wayside. Most of the seniors that came to St. Mary's had not seen a doctor or a dentist for many years.

Therefore, one of the first welcome resources that St. Mary's offered to the seniors was a visit to the Over-Sixty Health Center, a community clinic just for elders. Through networking, Over-Sixty and St. Mary's received federal healthcare through Alameda County Healthcare for the Homeless. This collaboration allowed for urgent care that was sensitive to the issues of homeless seniors. The doctors became aware of the special needs and worked closely with the social workers. This included outreach healthcare to the Drop-in Center and even to individuals in substandard housing or on the street. It also helped build that bond of trust between the homeless seniors and the healthcare professionals. This trust needs to be built before fearful homeless persons can get medical care.

Over-Sixty also provided dental care. The teeth of homeless seniors suffer greatly from lack of proper dental hygiene. Good dental care helps homeless seniors obtain proper nutrition because when they get needed dentures, they can eat a range of foods. Also, when the seniors receive dentures, it improves their appearance and self-esteem. One senior showed up at the Center and said with pride, "Did you notice my new teeth?"

Difficult To Ask for Help

Seniors find it very difficult to ask to help. This unfortunate story shows the fierce independence of these elders:

> One senior who was developmentally disabled began to show serious signs of being unable to care for himself. Though he was only functioning on an eight-year-old mental level and was eighty years old, he prided himself

> on living independently. One day he fell in his room. After decades of independence, he did not call out for help. When someone did come to his room, he did not even ask for help to get up. It was two days later before someone realized he was not just resting on the floor but could not get up. When we did get him to Over-Sixty Health Center, the physician discovered he had developed Parkinson's disease.

This is an extreme example, but this desire to make it on their own and not be "on the dole" is firmly in the minds of most seniors of all economic brackets. Many seniors will go through great personal suffering and hide their needs rather than ask for help. This desire to be independent is another reason why outreach to homeless seniors is so important. Sometimes the worker must build trust and educate the elders to even convince them to apply for their earned Social Security. Much greater encouragement by the worker is needed for a senior to apply for GA (see note 3) or SSI (see note 14). After the worker assures the seniors, "You have a right to food and shelter for your needs," some seniors permit the worker to help them with their basic needs.

Surviving Till I Get Social Security—Reading

I am sixty some and living on the street.
I can survive.
I keep myself clean.
I go down to Lake Merritt in a sheltered spot each day and wash myself.
I wear dark clothes and wash off the outside of them when they get dirty.
I worked many years.
I'm waiting until I am sixty-five to get my Social Security.
I hurt my back lifting a boulder so it does not bend quite right.
I live near the railroad track.
I am quiet and no one notices me much.
I clean up around a few places for people.
They give me a few dollars.
I collect some cans and get some more money.
I am surviving.
I am waiting until I am sixty-five to get my Social Security.

Ageism

In American society where production is equated with a person's "worth," there is discrimination against those who are older. Corporations cut costs by eliminating the higher-paid workers and those close to retirement. There is a sense that seniors are a "throw away" group. This ageism also lowers some senior's sense of self-worth. Helping homeless seniors value their lives and develop goals for themselves was part of St. Mary's challenge.

RESPONDING TO THE NEEDS OF SENIORS

Move More Slowly

When I first came to St. Mary's, I had limited experience working with seniors. My director, Carol Cook, said that the majority of what we know about people applies to seniors, "Just move more slowly." The physical reactions of the body slow as people age, so whether it is getting into a car or moving down the street, things all take a little longer.

Assistance With the System

Whether it is applying for Social Security or applying for housing, many seniors have no experience with the process and feel overwhelmed. Step-by-step education, support, and, at times, accompaniment are needed to assist the senior to move their plans smoothly ahead.

Support Groups

Seniors easily become isolated. First of all, isolation provides a form of protection. Other factors that contribute to the seniors' isolation are deaths of family and friends. Many seniors, through a sense of shame in being homeless, separate from their families and churches. Because as retirees they do not have work contacts, their opportunities for mutual-sharing are limited. Homeless seniors are also often shunned by other seniors at senior centers because of their inability to keep up their hygiene.

To overcome this isolation, it is extremely important that senior programs build community. This was done at St. Mary's through the Drop-in Center, support groups, and integration into senior homeless community programs. The homeless seniors at St. Mary's considered the opportunity to have friendly conversation the greatest asset of the program.

Finding Their Value

I once heard a Latino man on a radio talkshow speak of elders in the Latino/a community as a source of history and of balance. The challenge of the homeless senior program at St. Mary's was to build for the seniors a sense of self-worth through sharing ideas and experiences. The success of the endeavor was present in the statement of a formerly homeless woman who became a volunteer and said, "We have our experience to share." The support groups where each senior shared on a topic reinforced the fact that seniors have wisdom to share. St. Mary's art project "Building Connections" in which the seniors and fourth graders did art collages of their lives and dreams gavc the seniors another experience of sharing their wisdom.

Seniors have many skills that build up through the years. When they are invited to tap those skills in projects, it builds the community and enhances the seniors' quality of life. At St. Mary's, a former engineer helped with another person's plumbing and taught leatherwork to seniors. Those with cooking skills delighted all at picnics and parties. Other seniors volunteered and benefited the program and themselves through record keeping, computer skills, receptionist work, writing advocacy letters and grants, dramatic presentations, and music and art.

Often, people who have overcome personal problems and dealt with many of life issues have much to teach others in a program. The seniors who were recovering from addiction and other mental disorders gave much to the program in personal witness and education of others. They, too, were strengthened in the process.

Opportunities for Enrichment Activities

Seniors frequently have time on their hands. To have profitable activities that stimulate their minds and imaginations, as well as incorporate old and new experiences provides new learning and great enrichment. To provide a community where the seniors can plan activities and outings together expands their world. Encouragement, education, and transportation all are necessary for this.

Transportation bears underlining. Many seniors—because of economic and health reasons—do not have their own car. Transportation is a factor that must be considered in any senior project. Also, because of special disabilities, many seniors cannot use public transportation. St. Mary's Homeless Senior Program has the flexibility of all staff providing transportation for seniors to services and activities. For some senior aides and volunteers, their key activity was to provide transportation. Helping seniors access transportation through senior bus passes, and medical releases from doctors for taxi vouchers was part of early stabilization. Any senior program must consider transportation a basic need.

THE GIFTS OF SENIORS

Deep Sense of Spirituality

One of the gifts that seniors contribute is a deep sense of spirituality. As J said, "It is only that belief that gets you through." Even the most mentally confused senior openly volunteered that it was a Higher Power that helped them to survive on the streets.

The seniors do not hesitate to speak freely in front of others of their spiritual convictions and their faith. This sharing is a source of mutual encouragement and edification.

Wisdom

Seniors have a great wisdom to share. For example, military veterans spoke of how they had changed since they were young soldiers. They saw firsthand how the horrors of war affected everyone, especially the civilians. They no longer saw war as a solution.

Deep Gratitude

Seniors expressed a sense of "wanting to give back" for what they had received. The strength of the peer activities in the St. Mary's community was a result of the seniors wanting to contribute back for the support and services received. This circular effect deeply enhances the individuals and a program. The atmosphere created by this spirit is very positive and contagious.

Gifts To Give—Poem

I have gifts to give.
I can pound a nail,
  escort another senior shopping.
I can type 60 words a minute,
  and answer a phone.
I can make things with my hands,
  and they can raise hearts and money.

I can read to a child,
dramatize the "Night Before Christmas."
I can pray and *do* pray
each night for this sad world.
I can fix your sink,
and tell a legislator the needs of homeless seniors.
I can share my ideas,
lead a group,
and plan an activity.
I can smile and be
the best *me*.
I could not do most of these things
when on the streets,
but I can do more now I am inside.
I thank God each day I have a home,
and I help out at St. Mary's.

SKILL BUILDING—Valuing the gifts of seniors

✓ Invite a formerly homeless senior to discuss the difficulties they experienced being homeless.

✓ Think of famous people who as seniors are contributing to the world.

✓ Think of seniors that you know, for example, relatives, and try to imagine what they would do if they were homeless. Reflect on the following:
a) Their gifts that would be lost to you and others,
b) Their special vulnerabilities and how this would affect their ability to survive on the streets,
c) Their attitudes that would make it difficult for them to access needs.

✓ Notice the commercials and movies on TV and their portrayal of seniors. How does this affect the treatment of seniors and their role in our society?

SUMMARY

Homeless seniors have special difficulties that include: physical vulnerability on the streets, healthcare needs, difficulty in asking for help, and the prejudice of the American society against the aged.

The majority of what we know about people applies to seniors, but seniors do move more slowly and need more assistance to get through the system to obtain Social Security or housing. The assistance is education, support, and sometimes accompaniment. Homeless seniors are especially isolated so they benefit from support groups and other ways of building community.

Seniors need to find their value. When seniors are invited to tap their many skills in projects, it builds the community and enhances the quality of their lives. Seniors often have time on their hands. To have profitable activities that stimulate their minds and imaginations, as well as incorporate old and new experiences, provides new learning and great enrichment.

Any senior program must consider transportation a basic need.

Seniors have certain gifts that include: a deep sense of spirituality, a great wisdom to share, and a sense of "wanting to give back" for what they have received.

Skill-building exercises that focus on the needs and the value of seniors are included.

CHAPTER 9 *HOMELESS SENIOR WOMEN*

To Be Out on the Street—Reading

To be out on the street without shelter or warmth or protection …
To be out on the street, to be seventy years old …
To be out on the street, to be seventy, and to be blinded by cataracts …
To be out on the street, to be seventy, to be blinded by cataracts, and to be a woman …
To be out on the street, to be seventy, to be blinded by cataracts, to be a woman, and to be mentally disoriented …
To be out on the street, to be seventy, to be blinded by cataracts, to be a woman, to be mentally disoriented, and to be addicted to alcohol to quell the fear, shame, and chaotic thinking …
It staggers the mind to grasp the ordeal of a senior woman on the street … unless that person is you.

VULNERABILITY OF HOMELESS SENIOR WOMEN

Seniors who are homeless are vulnerable, but senior women—as any woman instinctively realizes—are most vulnerable. Homeless women can be, and are, sexually abused and exist in fear for their very lives. One woman who lived in her car said, "To sleep in the car overnight is not good because it is very dangerous. [The male abusers] are looking for women who are alone, and they prey on women in that situation."

Fear that escalates to terror is a dominant emotion of senior women who are at risk or who are homeless. The trauma of homelessness interferes further with their ability to function and take care of personal needs. Because of their vulnerability to physical attacks from men, senior women find places to live that are open to public view. The woman described in the above passage, "To Be Out on the Streets," lived at night in a bus shelter in the heart of the city. There were streetlights and a 24-hour newsstand near her bus shelter. Buses and police came by most of the night.

Some senior women, as do younger women, pair up on the street with a homeless man in order to have a protector. The relationship itself may not be safe, and the man may be taking more than his share of the funds; but some women feel forced to choose this over being alone and unprotected.

Filled With Shame

Society places an extra burden on women in terms of morals and appearance. Women who are addicted are judged by a different standard than men. Women internalize these deprecating societal norms. Women also feel a special shame if they cannot take care of their personal needs or hygiene. The difficulty of homeless women to take care of personal toiletry needs creates special embarrassment. A formerly homeless senior woman's comments are as follows:

> [It is] different for women because women need access to a restroom that a man does not need. It was very difficult to find a place to go to a restroom. A lot of filling stations will not let you use restrooms if you don't buy gas. Nobody gives a damn if the poor are inconvenienced. It is hard to deal with the attitude. It is not hard to understand because of the emphasis on the almighty dollar.

Senior women more often have bladder difficulties that result in lack of bladder control. There is shame around this that causes some senior women to avoid doctors. If the bladder condition becomes serious, it also may make it difficult to maintain their independence in living. One homeless senior woman needed encouragement to have breast tumors checked out. Some women's shame around their personal needs drives them away from the very medical attention needed to resolve the problem.

I think that women tend to personalize their situation more. They think it is their fault that they are homeless rather than the result of special circumstances or a failure on the part of society. This self-blame leads senior women to isolation and great sensitivity about their predicament.

Harriet's Story

> After the death of my husband I could not face living alone .... I moved in with my daughter. I did not mourn. I threw myself into my job. I had a master's in counseling and for the last 9 1/2 years was an administrator over 13 staff and 48 residential clients. I lost my job. I did not fight it. My daughter was not happy having me. I was not old enough for the senior complexes—I was 61. I used my little savings on my husband's funeral. I had no options. My daughter gave me an ultimatum of moving out by April. I began to feel alone. I was so frightened—so frightened. I saw myself not having a place to live. I saw myself being outdoors on a park bench.
>
> I was very ashamed. I felt fear, shame, guilt—I thought I brought it on myself. I should not have lost my job. I should have fought for it. [It was] so shameful because I [thought I] should not be in this situation. I did not go to my church. I was too ashamed that my daughter was treating me the way she did. I did not tell anyone until it was over. I felt guilty. It was my fault. I thought there was something I could or should have done to prevent this from happening.

Shame keeps the secret hidden and intensifies the problem. Senior women's stories of homelessness are often untold because of shame. Of the one hundred or more senior women I assisted, only a handful would testify to the hardships of homelessness in front of others. When I asked them if they would share their story, some would only do so if they could keep their anonymity. Some women fear that their relatives will know that they were homeless. Others will not relate their story at all because they want to distance themselves from the experience.

Accustomed To Be Caregivers

Women in most societies, especially older women, are accustomed to the role of caring for others. At the same time, they are dependent on others for decisions and finances. Harriet explained this. "All my life I helped other people. Here, when *I* needed help I was ashamed. I forgot where the resources were. All that went out of my mind." Harriet had a master's in counseling, and for years as part of her job she helped ex-felons to obtain housing and other resources; yet she was unable to help herself. I found this occurred with a number of senior women who were professional caregivers.

Financially Unaware

Some women, especially in a household where the male is very dominating, are financially naive. The women are not allowed to ask questions. Senior women may not know how to manage their finances when their husbands die. If the woman's partner is abusive and she decides to leave, she may not have sufficient funds for herself and her dependents.

One formerly homeless woman tells about women's financial difficulties:

> Women lose their houses because they can't pay the note or can't get a 2nd mortgage. They lost their husbands and lost their jobs. Older women [workers] used to be considered valuable. Not so now. Companies are trying to cut down on paying health or retirement benefits. Savings are gone before long. [They] lose their home and they don't have anything.

SKILL BUILDING—Sensitivity to senior women

- ✓ If possible invite a woman who was at risk or was homeless to tell her story.
- ✓ Recall a time when you were emotionally burdened by a death, accident, a job loss, or even a lingering cold or a severe burn on the hand, for example. Remember the emotional vulnerability, the irritability, and lack of coping mechanisms for tasks that you ordinarily did with great ease. Recall how the vulnerability often led to other difficulties. Share this with your group.
- ✓ This is a mental exercise that is to be kept personal (or shared as you wish). Recall a situation that you do not want to share with others and the shame that causes that reluctance. Note how this shame always has an aspect of self-deprecation. How does shame affect a homeless senior woman's efforts to stabilize herself?

ISOLATION AND SENSE OF HELPLESSNESS

The vicious cycle for senior women is isolation and a sense of helplessness and depression. It is commonly known that depression is anger held inward. Because women tend to be socialized toward withholding their anger, this may account for more depression among women. Isolation among homeless senior women is common.

Harriet tells of her experience of depression:

> I was very unhappy. I thought death would be better than this. You are boxed in. Each way I turned, I walked into concrete walls. One day, I rang the doorbell at a senior complex (at this time I was 62) and asked for housing. They just answered over the intercom that the waiting list was years long. They would not even come to the door. I cried. I thought about suicide for the first time in my life.

WOMEN'S SUPPORT GROUP

Safety Primary

Although, St. Mary's Homeless Senior Program has 30 to 40 percent women, only about 10 percent of them would attend the general support group. It was thought that the women did not feel safe or were too shamed to be with the men. Therefore, with the help of some of the women, the workers initiated a senior woman's support group.

Overcoming the Isolation

The group was itself set up to overcome the isolation that is part of the senior women's way of dealing with fear, shame, guilt, and depression. Overcoming the isolation was a great hurdle. It took much one-on-one support and encouragement to bring the women out. Telephone contact by workers and some of the women and transportation were a *must* to keep the women involved. The emotional frailty of some women was such that being asked to come on the bus rather than to be picked up was a signal, "You are not wanted." Without a great effort and commitment by the workers and volunteers, the homeless senior women's group would not have stabilized.

Building Self-esteem and a Sense of Their Beauty

From the beginning, the support group had as its centerpiece activity a breakfast tea. There were fancy napkins, attractive plates, and other table decorations. The purpose was to say, "This is beautiful because you are beautiful." For special occasions, the breakfast was held at a private home or meeting rooms with special dishes and decorations. Both staff and women took the opportunity to dress up. Photos were taken.

Activities, such as readings from publications that affirmed aging women, meditation, personal sharing, and dance movement were well received. A balance between sharing and taking trips was important. Trips to the Black Women's Photo Exhibition in the local museum, an art show on abuse and women, and trips to the botanical flower gardens were enjoyed by the women. Sharing about their feelings, however, was very difficult because of the women's lack of self-esteem. But they appreciated the companionship and slowly learned to overcome some of these difficult communication barriers. A few women who attended and experienced the openness of 12-step groups modeled for the other women how to trust and share.

Empowerment

The empowerment of the individual woman was encouraged through participation. Participation in decision-making, planning, preparing, carrying out the program, and evaluating made the group really belong to the women themselves. Because women are trained so well to be caregivers, women workers and volunteers, as well as a few of the natural leaders, can perpetuate the disempowerment of the women. To keep drawing the women into participation allows them to own the great power that is theirs.

SKILL BUILDING—Evaluating if your caretaking is empowering.

Answer each statement: 4 Always 3 Sometimes 2 Seldom 1 Never

1. How often do I do things for others that are my idea not theirs?
2. How often do I get in conflict because of this caretaking?
3. Was I affirmed as a child for taking care of others' needs?
4. Did I take on a caregiver role with my parents?
5. Do I feel better doing something for others rather than teaching them to do it for themselves?
6. Do I feel better doing things myself rather than delegating?
7. Are most of my relationships based on taking care of the other person?

If the total score is 20 or more, you might need to move toward more empowering practices. Books on codependency, 12-step Codependence Anonymous, other groups, and therapy all can help develop a more empowering style of relating.

SUMMARY

It staggers the mind to grasp the ordeal of a senior woman on the street. All women instinctively realize that it is unsafe for women to be homeless. Women can be, and are, sexually abused. Fear that escalates to terror is a dominant emotion of senior women who are at risk of homelessness or who are homeless. Because of their vulnerability to attacks, senior women find places that are open to public view to live.

Society places an extra burden on women in terms of appearance and morals. Homeless women also feel a special shame if they cannot take care of their personal needs or hygiene. The difficulty of homeless women to take care of personal toiletry needs creates special embarrassment. This shame leads the senior women to a common pattern of isolation and great sensitivity about their predicament. Some senior women have bladder difficulties that make it difficult to maintain their independence in living.

The vicious cycle for senior women is isolation and a sense of helplessness. Senior women's stories of homelessness are often untold because of shame.

Because at St. Mary's the women did not come to the general support group, it was assumed they felt ashamed or unsafe with the men. St. Mary's set up a group for the homeless senior women to overcome their isolation. It took much one-on-one support and encouragement to bring the women to the group. Building self-esteem and a sense of their beauty was key. The empowerment of the women was encouraged through participation.

A skill-building exercise to evaluate whether the worker's caretaking style encourages empowerment is included.

CHAPTER 10 *THE HOMELESS PERSON WITH ALCOHOL AND OTHER DRUG ADDICTION*

THE NEED FOR TREATMENT

Scientific understanding of addiction and treatment has grown significantly since the 1970s. Unfortunately, the nation's implementation of these findings for the general public has faltered. Education about the deadly danger of drug abuse is sporadic. While the number of persons with addiction needing treatment increased, the availability of affordable treatment declined. Accordingly, the number of homeless persons suffering from addiction also increased.

The worker in service agencies, shelters, and healthcare facilities encounters the homeless person who is addicted to drugs and alcohol. The worker's training about addiction varies from no training to advanced knowledge. The present chapter provides the worker with basic information in order to assist the homeless person who has addictions. Information on the correct attitude of the worker, the nature of addictions, methods of intervention, housing decisions, and follow-up are included (see also Chapter 3, How to Assess for Addiction). The application of money management is explained. Special information on work with homeless seniors with addictions is presented. Skill-building intervention exercises are also included.

THE WORKER'S ATTITUDE TOWARD THE PERSON WITH AN ADDICTION

The worker's respect for the dignity of the person suffering from an addiction fosters empathy and empowerment in the relationship. The worker's respect develops through information and self-analysis. If the worker listens with an open mind to the story of those who are successfully overcoming their addiction, this can be a powerful education tool. It is important for the worker to examine through self-analysis fears and stereotypes about the person with an addiction.

SKILL BUILDING—Attitude toward the homeless person with an addiction

Invite a speaker who was homeless and addicted to share their recovery story.

Examining your attitude

Answer "Yes" or "No" to each of the attitude statements below:

1. I have a spontaneous negative reaction to anyone intoxicated. Yes/No
2. I believe that the addicted person freely chooses the addiction. Yes/No
3. I believe that the addicted person will never change. Yes/No
4. I believe that the homeless person who is addicted should be given the exact same services as someone who is homeless and not addicted. Yes/No
5. When the addicted person denies their addiction they are faking because it is obvious they know what they are choosing. Yes/No
6. A worker can tell whether a homeless person has an addiction by their appearance. Yes/No
7. If a person is homeless because of using money on their addiction, they deserve to be homeless. Yes/No
8. Older persons who are addicted abuse alcohol only. Yes/No
9. I think that older persons with an addiction find it harder to recover. Yes/No
10. I think an older person who is addicted should be allowed to live out their lives in comfort. No one should try to take away the little comfort this addiction provides. Yes/No

SKILL BUILDING—Changing your attitude

A group of workers tries to reflect honestly on the above statements and discusses how their attitudes influence how they relate to the homeless person who is addicted. If a worker responded "Yes" to any of the above statements, it indicates a need to examine the issue carefully. The information below corresponds numerically to the above attitude statements.

1. If you have a spontaneous negative reaction to a person who is intoxicated, realize that spontaneous reactions usually arise from personal experiences. Try to remember a strong negative experience of an intoxicated person and how the feeling from that event transferred to all persons who are intoxicated.

   A person with an addiction has a deadly problem. A person with, say, diabetes without medical treatment would die. A person with, say, heroin addiction, without treatment will also die. The addicted person does not benefit from rejection but needs caring, skillful intervention, treatment, and follow-up.

   In some circumstances and settings, a worker needs to tell an intoxicated person to leave voluntarily. If the person is out of control and threatening, the worker needs to call the police. The worker is enforcing a safety guideline. The intoxicated person, however, will usually realize when the worker's actions spring from antipathy.
2. It is not correct to simply say a person chooses an addiction. Factors which influence certain persons having an addiction are: heredity and body chemistry, family patterns, accessibility of drugs, and other bio-psycho-social factors.
3. A person who is addicted can change. Many people tell their stories of winning the day-to-day battle over addiction. Many live very full lives with the help of 12-step and other treatment programs.
4. To state that a worker should treat each homeless person the same, whether the person has an addiction or not, is to ignore the nature of addiction. For example, if a worker rents a room or a car to a person who is addicted this might be an invitation to destruction of the room, the car, the person, and others. To give a large sum of money to an addicted person can provide the means to commit suicide.

continued

SKILL BUILDING—Changing your attitude

5. For the worker to assume the homeless person who denies their addiction is faking, shows a lack of understanding of the nature of addiction. The addicted person does not actually realize they are addicted, especially in the earlier stages of the disorder. The addiction can be apparent to others but not to themselves. The individual must break through the denial for the healing process to start.
6. A worker cannot tell by appearances whether a homeless person has an addiction. If the person is intoxicated, the worker can suspect an addiction. The homeless person may have many ordinary problems, but in addition underneath this an addiction. In a few instances, I have worked with a person for several years and did not realize the person had an addiction. Personally, I found it hardest to realize that elderly women who had professional jobs all their lives could also have an addiction.
7. To deny services to homeless persons who have addictions is to deny that addiction is a mental disorder rather than a moral choice. The response must be one of awareness of the insidious and stubborn nature of addiction and knowledge that the addicted person needs proper help, not condemnation or neglect.
8. Among seniors, there is addiction to prescription drugs, street drugs, or alcohol.
9. Research does not indicate that an older person finds it harder to stop their addictive behavior. In my limited experience seniors tend to drink less than they did when they were younger. I feel the most important factor for recovery is that a person perceives there is something to win or lose from changing.
10. To say the older person should not have intervention or treatment is really the prejudice of ageism. Ageism causes the worker to look at the older person as not having much to give to the world. Ageism is prevalent in our society because many treatment programs do not accept individuals 60 years of age or older.

UNDERSTANDING DRUG AND ALCOHOL ADDICTION

Drug and alcohol addiction is a complex mental disorder. Initially the user of drugs wishes to stop *pain*. The development of the addiction is elusive. Hidden bio-psycho-social factors draw some persons more than others to an addiction. The addiction sneaks up on the person and their family. Together they deny for years that the addicted person is out of control.

As the craving for the drug or alcohol grows and financial resources dwindle, the addicted person slips into actions previously considered by themselves to be repulsive. Compelled by the psychological and physical craving, the addicted person can risk their job, steal from family and friends, desert a spouse and children, become homeless, or sell their bodies in the sex trade. The worker needs to be aware of the power of the addictive craving. The addicted homeless person who wants drugs or free housing can lie, manipulate, steal, plead, or burst into tears to get what they want. The worker armed with this realization must use critical thinking to do an objective assessment of each homeless person's needs (see Chapter 3, How to Assess for an Addiction). The worker needs to be alert to tendencies within themselves to rescue a homeless person with an addiction or to respond out of fear of displeasing (see Chapter 8, Over-identified Relationship). If the worker lends money to an addicted person, that money may be used for drugs and not be returned. If the worker uses a voucher to place in a hotel a person who is drinking uncontrollably—in a worst case scenario—the person may accidentally set a fire, cause their own death, and possibly the death of others:

> A few years ago, right before Thanksgiving, an alcoholic homeless senior from the St. Mary's Program relapsed and lost his housing. He received a voucher to a hotel from a county emergency service program. At the hotel, he continued drinking uncontrollably. While smoking a cigarette, he accidentally caused a fire that spread throughout the hotel. The fire killed him. Others barely escaped with their lives.

INTERVENTION

A worker with the homeless needs to become comfortable inquiring about addictions. Through role play (see Skill-Building—Confronting the addiction) the worker can overcome a natural reluctance and can ask the question, "How frequently do you use alcohol or drugs?" and can confront the homeless person on their choices. When a worker suspects a person does have an addiction, they note the level of denial to self or others. Strategies on the most effective intervention for this person, given their circumstances, are explored.

If I suspected in the first interview that the homeless person had an addiction, I invited them to the program in the following way:

> "Many of the people who come to us have addictions. We do not hold that against a person. We have in our program an addiction meeting on Monday's at 11:00 a.m. and a general support group on Thursday at 11:00 a.m. too. You can see if these meetings give you information that is helpful to you. Sometimes people realize that they need to work on certain issues in order to overcome their housing problems. We are here to help you. It is up to you."

The homeless person with an addiction needs to know the worker will not condemn them or give up on them because of their addiction. The worker conveys genuine and consistent concern by the message, "I am concerned for you and your health," or "I will work with you to get help when you want it." If the worker does not allow themselves to be manipulated and take up the slack, then perhaps later when the homeless person is in a crisis, they will come for assistance with their addiction.

The addicted person must take back responsibility for their life to overcome their addiction. In the first interview at the office, I asked the homeless person, "What do you want?" This question helped the person refocus their energy and desires. A person's deepest desires —not the surface ones like their addictions—(see Chapter 4, Desires) are the energy, which when tapped, moves the person back into a positive direction. Sometimes, this heart-to-heart discussion came at a time when the person was ready to do something to change their life. I assured them that I was on their team to help them achieve their authentic desires.

If, during the course of the interview, a person admitted an addiction, I affirmed them. "It is good that you *know* and can state what the problem is. This means you are on the right road. Now, you can start doing something about it. We can talk about what you need for your recovery." Together, we—the homeless person and I—determined a way to work toward recovery. Healing from an addiction is a lifelong process.

Some persons might be open to a treatment program. Determining eligibility and availability of programs are great hurdles to overcome.

When to work with the homeless person to get into a treatment can be important. At times, in the first interview when I was able to help an individual into an inpatient treatment program in another county, because of distance of the program, I lost contact with the person. Months later I encountered the person back on the streets. When as the referral service I was expected to provide the follow-up, I found it was better to first form the bond and get to know the person over a period of time before referring the person to treatment. When this extra work was done before referral, I found there was more likelihood that as the referral agency we could act as a support if the person wanted to link with our agency when the inpatient program was complete. With short-term treatment programs the continued support from the community agency is especially important.

Because an addiction develops over many years, the recovery process is also long. If an addicted person had this pattern for 20 years, it will take many years to get life fully back on course. The worker needs to have this long-range view. In the meantime the worker needs to notice and affirm small changes, such as, the person begins to sporadically come to see a worker or the person begins to share even a few ideas during a community activity.

Outreach and the Addicted Person

Outreach for the homeless addicted person can bring the person into a program. The addiction can keep the person in shame and isolation. Consistent outreach even if it is very brief can begin to be a deciding factor (see Chapter 1). The addicted person very often has mixed feelings about their substance abuse. This outreach can strengthen that part of the person that thinks that sobriety has more to offer than abuse.

Community As a Healing Force

If a worker invites the addicted homeless person into a healing community, they will have companions who can give an example of hope along the way to recovery. The community is the most stabilizing factor for recovery (see Chapter 6). The community can do much more than just the individual worker. The Drop-in Center and the support groups at St. Mary's Program often attracted and drew in the homeless person who was addicted. Program participants always evaluated the community as the most helpful source.

HOUSING DECISIONS

Frequently, I said to a person, "A landlord does not want a person who is drunk publicly and makes it difficult for the other tenants. Someone who is drinking is a hazard because they can fall down and hurt themselves. You have to make a *choice* whether you want permanent housing or whether you want to keep on drinking. It is your choice but I hope that you want to make it, because I would like you to have good housing and be healthy and safe." If the worker is caring and yet does not try to exert control (see Chapter 4, Who Wants It: The Worker or the Homeless Person), this leaves the addicted person free to respond to the situation and not to the personality or wishes of the worker.

When the persons I worked with chose sobriety and permanent housing then I worked first with them on their individual recovery plan. I asked the person to come to addiction and support groups and frequent one-on-one meetings. I helped the person find a place in a shelter or temporary housing until they had some time in recovery.

A lack of supportive transitional housing for homeless persons with an addiction was and still is a great problem. It was difficult to place a person in a hotel in the area where their old friends hung out. Often when I placed the person—who was new in their sobriety—in a hotel I leaned on their relationship with our program. I underlined how important it was take responsibility as a tenant. This often seemed to work. When it did not, I worked with the person who relapsed to get help. If they chose not to get help and needed to be evicted because of disruptive behavior or for not paying their rent, I appealed to the person to leave voluntarily rather than causing the manager to incur court costs. A few times, a manager had to take the person to court to get them out, but hopefully managers saw that there were other tenants we placed who were successful in continuing their recovery.

A homeless person in the program had to have some recovery time before I worked with them on permanent housing. I learned this the hard way. If the leverage of getting housing was gone, the addicted person—with little or no recovery—felt no need to work on their addiction.

Months of nonpayment of rent and unsafe behavior for themselves and other tenants was the result in several instances.

If the person who relapsed comes for help, the worker can use this crisis to strengthen the recovery plan. The worker might use the person's desire to keep their housing as an incentive for them to choose to enter a treatment program, inpatient or outpatient. (The worker intervenes to save the housing if possible only *after* the person has actually entered the program.) Or, in another case at some point in their recovery, a person's easy access to their check might be too great a temptation. The worker can agree to lend monies to them to save their housing *after* the person enters a money-management program (see Chapter 4, Loan Fund).

The following tragedy occurred when an addiction was not properly addressed:

> St. Mary's assisted a senior woman who drank heavily to get permanent housing without addressing her addiction. As soon as she had permanent housing, she hid away in her apartment and refused all contact. She drank heavily in her solitude. First, she broke her hip. Then, she set her apartment on fire. She died in the fire.

MONEY MANAGEMENT

Money management is an important avenue to assisting the homeless person especially those with addictions (and other mental disorders or both). Of course, money—especially someone else's—is always a tricky problem. A person is understandably leery that the worker might want to manipulate them out of their money. And for a person with an addiction to give someone control of their money, is a big step. Money is an avenue to their drug or alcohol. To convince someone that money management is necessary, I used the following argument:

> "I know that you really want to get *your* check in your own name, but it is not working. *Your money* is only *your money* but it is meant to be spent on housing, food, and clothing for you. It is your choice, but there is only one way that I can go to bat for you with that manager. You did not pay your rent and I will assist you with that rent only if I know the loan will be paid back. Also I need to

> know that your money will be used on your rent in the future. So I will pay this rent, if you agree to have money management. That way the rent and bills are paid at the beginning of the month and you will get the rest of the money on a schedule that you and your payee work out."

For a social services agency to provide money management has pluses and minuses. I found that for a person with whom I had formed a bond and who was very frightened and fragile, our agency was the *only* one the person could trust. On the other hand, a number of homeless persons were angry about being forced by a possible future landlord to accept money management. If another agency did the money management in these anger-provoking instances, the homeless person could accept St. Mary's case management.

FOLLOW-UP

Consistent follow-up is integral to a recovery program. The bond of trust needs to be further strengthened while the person with an addiction learns the new tools for coping with life. For the person with an addiction to stay in the local community while they learn the new skills of living sober is daunting. Scheduled one-on-one weekly meetings allow the person to continue to explore their issues. Attendance at the addiction meeting and other groups is essential. A drop-in center or day program can provide critical support.

Because most workers have excessively large caseloads, the worker has difficulty staying on top of situations. It is not sufficient for the worker to respond only to crises. It is important that a program have volunteers or have some way of providing follow-up.

A relapse is one of the hazards of addiction. The worker cannot rescue the person who relapsed. The worker can let the person know when they encounter them that the worker is there to assist them when they are ready. Staying with the person in this way for years can pay off. Often the person, especially if a senior, ends up with health crises and realizes that they need to choose to be sober. Sometimes, circumstances choose for the person. The addicted person can fall and break their hip. They can be in a nursing home temporarily or permanently. Once there, they may have no access to alcohol.

Some families have to place an alcoholic relative under conservatorship through probate court. The following are reasons for conservatorship: the person is clearly dangerous to self and others or cannot make their own decisions. Persons with alcoholism and alcohol dementia (see Chapter 11) or other mental disorders may meet these requirements.

HOMELESS SENIORS AND DRUG AND ALCOHOL ADDICTIONS

MH's Story

> I drank for 40 years. My father was light [African American] and he drank. My mother didn't. All four light children drank. The others looked liked my mother and didn't. I was drinking in Chicago. Sunday I'd have $200. Wednesday, would come, I wouldn't have a dime. I didn't know how I spent it. I was going backwards. Alcohol is a stick-up artist. It robs you of clothes, money, and relationships. I was homeless.
>
> When I came back out here to California where I grew up, I didn't want people to see me this way. I thought it was a good reason [to quit]. At first I kept trying to do it myself. I failed every week.
>
> I was close to the VA because so many [buddies of mine] were killed in the Korean War. So, I went to the vets to get cleaned up. I've been going to the VA for eight years. For me the trick is I have to keep going for support. I don't feel I am strong enough to do it on my own. I don't want to take that chance.
>
> I was displaced by the earthquake. I came to St. Mary's who found housing for me. I help with the Monday [alcohol] meeting [at St. Mary's] because it helps me. Some people are helped because they are around someonc who is sober. I want everyone to have what I have.
>
> I really enjoy life to the fullest. It is all new. Sometimes you feel that you are just out of jail after 50 years. Such a great feeling! So free.

> Older people need to quit drinking sooner. It is especially dangerous for the older person for themselves and others. [Being sober] is important until a person draws his last breath.

MH was the recipient in '93 of "The Points of Light Award" by the Komen Breast Cancer Foundation for his volunteer work for five years of helping lead the alcoholism program at St. Mary's Homeless Senior Program. His art is displayed in this book (pp. 88 and 148) .

St. Mary's Homeless Senior Addiction Program

St. Mary's Homeless Senior Program in its first year found that 70 to 80 percent of the homeless seniors in its program had a history of drug and alcohol addiction. Addiction treatment is integral to work with homeless persons, including the work with seniors. Therefore, early on St. Mary's incorporated a weekly addiction meeting into its program. In 1994, the program received a grant to expand its outpatients' addiction program for seniors.

One of the ways that seniors relate differently than younger people to addiction was noted by Georgia, a current worker at St. Mary's. Many seniors see drug abuse as a moral issue rather than as a mental disorder. I was reminded of this when one of the seniors referred to his time of abusing alcohol as when he was a bad person.

Prescription Drug Abuse

Prescription drug abuse is common for seniors. These seniors receive drugs from their regular doctor and without the regular doctor's knowledge go to other doctors, and/or emergency rooms. The abuse may be so severe that it endangers their health. During my years of work for low-income seniors in the Oakland area there were no programs that provided safe medical detox and treatment. This true story illustrated the difficulty:

> My first intervention with prescription drugs was with Tom, a 62-year-old senior with a long history of addiction which included the tranquilizer Halcion. Tom used to live in his car but recently he convinced a social service agency to assist him to get into senior housing. Tom started to fall behind on his rent. That is when I realized why he was always out of money.

I offered help to Tom by saying, “Don’t you want more for your life?” Tom said he did. On the advice of a consultant we went to the emergency room of the general hospital. Eleven hours later, the doctor practically laughed at us. “We do not even assist those with heroin withdrawal.” The next morning Tom and I called outpatient detox programs. They said Tom was a medical risk, and they could not take the responsibility. Tom was having symptoms of withdrawal from the prescription drugs. He left the office in a panic probably to look for more drugs. Since then, Tom has had serious medical crises. During one crisis, Tom went for treatment for a time. When the crisis passed, he returned to his addiction.

SKILL BUILDING—Confronting the addiction

✓ Form a fishbowl with two workers in the center and the others around the outside. Do a role play with the two workers: 1) the homeless person and 2) the worker. The scenario is an at-risk-homeless man who comes to the office and asks the worker for rent money because he said that someone had stolen his money. Upon questioning he claims this has happened each of the past three months and periodically before that. After the role play, share feelings. Discuss as a group: intervention, treatment, and housing arrangements.

✓ Form groups of two: 1) the homeless person and 2) the worker. Now role play:

a) A visit with a woman who lives in her car and somehow her money never stretches enough lately for housing. Discuss money management and treatment.

b) An interview with someone who comes into the office after being released from the hospital for severe liver damage from alcohol abuse. The person is too sick to be out-of-doors. Discuss money management and housing.

c) A talk on the street with a senior who is a veteran and admits he has been drinking and using drugs most of his life. His health is failing. Discuss: the feelings during the interview, effective means of intervention, treatment goals and follow-up.

Senior Women and Addiction

Alcohol and drug addiction has special features for homeless senior women. The safety and shame that are particular to homeless women are intensified if there is alcohol or drug addiction. Women isolate themselves and, therefore, can use more and larger quantities of a drug before intervention takes place. Their health suffers more. As a worker I found myself most in denial about homeless senior women and their addiction.

A senior woman Lovie (see Chapter 1, Lovie's Story) taught me that people can never be given up on. Lovie said she drank for years. "I'd drink every day if I could get it. I said the only way I would stop drinking is if they stopped making it." Lovie was proud she was able to stop drinking.

SUMMARY

If the worker listens with an open mind to the stories of those who are successfully overcoming their addiction, it can be a powerful educational tool.

Drug and alcohol addiction is a very complex and powerful disease with an elusive development. The worker needs to be able to note clues that may indicate an addiction (see Chapter 3, How to Assess for an Addiction) and to be able to comfortably ask the homeless person questions about their possible addiction. In order to intervene with the addicted person the worker needs a supportive and yet objective attitude. The worker's success may depend on outreach to the homeless person on the streets, motivating the person to get in touch with their positive desires for their future, and referral to appropriate treatment services. The worker's skilled use of permanent housing, money management, and consistent follow-up in a supportive community are integral to the person's recovery.

The worker needs to be aware of the reality of prescription drug abuse, frequently found among seniors, and the serious personal health problems that result from women with addictions who isolate themselves for many years.

Role-play exercises are included.

CHAPTER 11 *THE HOMELESS PERSON WITH A MENTAL DISORDER OR A DUAL DIAGNOSIS*

People, I Hide From You—Poem

Don't see me, people!
You frighten me.
Frighten me like
  my stepfather who crept
  to my bedroom at night.
People, go away. GO AWAY.
Oh, today I am calmer—
  a little.
I want my check.
I want food. I haven't
  eaten anything but half a candy bar
  and leftover chicken scraps for two days.
Yes, today, I'll take your quarter.
Don't talk! Don't stare at me!
I'm human.
Oh, I wear a hard hat.
Once this man hit
  me on the head.
I want my check.
No! I won't sign.
People steal from you
  when you sign. They lock you up.
I want my check.
No! I won't sign.
I used to be on medicine
  in the hospital at Napa.
In Napa there were no voices.
In Oakland I hear many voices.
I played a musical
  instrument in high school;
I got good grades.
Then they said I cracked.
Go away! Help me!

You see at times I say things I
don't mean.
I can't help it.
Be kind. Don't frighten me.
I want my check. I'm hungry.
My family? At least they do not
know this is me.

WORKING WITH A HOMELESS PERSON WITH A MENTAL DISORDER

Because of the national policy of closing many of the state mental hospitals and not funding community mental health, persons with a mental disorders frequently are forced into homelessness. Seniors are among the homeless persons with mental disorders.

The worker in service agencies, shelters, and especially those doing outreach encounter the homeless person with a mental disorder (or several mental disorders at the same time). Because the worker might have little or no training in understanding mental disorders, this chapter provides basic information.

This chapter deals first with the worker's attitude toward the person with a mental disorder. It goes on to describe some mental disorders that frequently occur among the homeless. Stories of a person with this disorder being housed are included.

Addictions, which are a type of mental disorder, can occur at the same time as other mental disorders. This is referred to, in lay terms, as dual diagnosis. Some basic ways to assist the dual-diagnosed homeless person are recommended.

The manifestation of mental disorders can differ in the aging process. Because my work was with homeless seniors, some of the pertinent differences of mental disorders as they occur in seniors are presented.

ATTITUDES TOWARD THE HOMELESS PERSON WITH A MENTAL DISORDER

The attitude of the worker toward the person with a mental disorder determines the quality of their relationship. The worker through education and self-analysis can enhance their respect for the dignity of the mentally disabled homeless person. With increased understanding, the worker can more easily develop an empowering empathetic relationship.

SKILL BUILDING—Attitude toward the person with a mental disorder

Have a formerly homeless person who suffered from a mental disorder(s) which possibly includes an addiction tell their experience of homelessness and how things were able to change for them.

Examining your attitudes

Answer "Yes" or "No" to each of the attitude statements below.

1. I can determine that a person has a mental disorder by their external appearance. Yes/No
2. The person with a mental disorder has lower intellectual capacity than others, so I need to speak more loudly and slowly to them. Yes/No
3. I cannot trust the person with a mental disorder to know their own needs because of their inability to think. Yes/No
4. I feel that those who hear voices and run away from people on the street are too far gone to offer anything again either to themselves, their families or the community. Yes/No
5. I think that if the homeless person with a mental disorder only has housing, food, and shelter, they will be well. Yes/No
6. The person with a mental disorder who is "out of reality" does not suffer the same way as other people. Yes/No
7. I feel the homeless person with a mental disorder has nothing to offer me or the community in spiritual wisdom. Yes/No
8. I am uneasy and frightened when relating to those with obvious mental disorders. Yes/No
9. I feel that only psychologists can communicate with a person with a mental disorder. Yes/No
10. All homeless persons with a mental disorders need to be placed permanently in locked mental hospitals. Yes/No

***SKILL BUILDING*—Changing your attitudes.**

A group of workers try to reflect honestly on the above statements and discuss how their attitudes influence how they relate to the homeless person with a mental disorder. If a worker responded "Yes" to any of the above statements, this indicates a need to examine that statement carefully. The following chart has information corresponding numerically to the above attitude statements to facilitate discussion.

1. The external appearance of a person might give no clue to the internal confusion, desperation, or loss of cognitive functioning. It might be only through listening carefully to the person's perceptions, personal history, and, if possible, outside information, that the worker can understand the mental disorder. Often, it takes a number of contacts to have an effective understanding. It is important for the worker to realize that the person's inner world can be filled with mental distress that I compare to earthquakes. This inner world of mental stress usually must be tended to before a person's life can be stabilized.
2. A mental disorder may have no direct relationship to intelligence. A person can be brilliant and have the disorder of paranoia or delusions. On the other hand, the disorder can affect a person's intellectual thinking in a limited or an extensive way. Therefore, the worker needs to adjust their communication so that the homeless person really understands. Anyone with any type of disorder is often hypersensitive to disrespectful treatment, such as being spoken down to or hearing workers talking about them as if they were not present.
3. Because the homeless person with a mental disorder can be very aware of their needs, it is important that they are listened to and that their comments are taken seriously. You can learn a great deal. Outside verification might be needed if the disorder affects the person's ability to make mental judgments.
4. Because the person with a mental disorder may have profound intellectual and spiritual insights, they can—in spite of and because of their illness—offer much to the community. When Lovie Burkes (see Chapter 1) was under psychiatric care, she shared her inner riches as deepened by her experiences.

continued

SKILL BUILDING—Changing your attitudes

5. Besides needing the basic necessities of food, clothing, and shelter, the person with a mental disorder possibly needs medication to clarify their confused thinking. For example, a person can need medication for mental disorders caused by neurochemical reactions such as hearing voices or depression.
6. The person with a mental disorder who hears voices and so forth does suffer excruciating mental pain. There are many self-reports that document the anguish of those with mental disorders. In reality, the person with a mental disorder are more easily traumatized by homelessness, because of their limited ability to cope with stress and of their vulnerability to others. Sometimes persons with drug addictions find them easy prey.
7. Just as you would discern the spiritual veracity of any other person you would do the same with the spiritual comments of the homeless person. (Homeless persons, whether they had mental disorders or not, taught me a great deal of spiritual truth by their faith and wisdom.)
8. In relating initially with the person with mental disorders, the worker can easily feel some anxiety. Understanding that the person with a mental disorder (see Chapter 3) experiences *ordinary* human feelings with *extraordinary* intensity helps to ease some of the insecurity of the new worker. When the worker meets a person with mental disorders, this can raise fears that this disorder can happen to them also. If the worker is not consciously aware of this fear, they can categorize the person as different and desire to distance themselves.
9. If the worker feels that only a psychologist can communicate with the person with a mental disorder, then the worker will not feel capable of providing assistance. Sensitive listening is the beginning for anyone to understand the needs of the other person. By listening, a worker can find out how the person sees the world and then address their needs. The worker does not have to have all the titles and degrees to be flexible and creative in communicating with someone who has a unique way of coping with their reality. For example, the sensitive worker may need to let a paranoid person drag a cart *wherever* they go.

continued

SKILL BUILDING—Changing your attitudes

10. The homeless person with a mental disorder does not need to be locked up permanently in a mental hospital. The health needs of persons with mental disorders vary. Basic mental health services should include outreach, medical evaluation and assistance, availability of hospitalization for assessment and stabilization, medication, consistent case workers, counseling, and community supports.

ASSESSING MENTAL STATE

Chapter 3 provides a general approach to understanding the homeless person and assessing their mental state. If the worker answers the mental status questions, these can supply information that indicates the person may have one or more of the psychiatric disorders listed below. This list includes only broad groups that are commonly found among homeless persons (DSM-IV[20]).

Psychotic Disorders

Psychotic disorders affect the ability of the person to relate to the same reality most people experience.

Schizophrenia is a disorder in which people sometimes actually see, hear, and smell things that the outside observer does not perceive. Persons with schizophrenia are often hypersensitive to outside stimuli. Their inner interpretation of all this bombardment of stimuli is very confusing and can make concentration, remembering, and organizing their ideas very difficult. Sometimes they do know who they are, where they are, and what time of the year it is. The disorientation can be ongoing or recurrent. Recurrent means that it can be present for a number of months and then the thoughts processes clear for a time. Typically the person has little control over these experiences. Being homeless and without resources adds greatly to the confusion. Some persons try to overcome the loss of orientation by making files and writing copious notes to themselves.

One type of schizophrenia is the *paranoid type*. The worker might wonder if the homeless person suffers from paranoia if the person is very fearful and cannot be approached openly on the street. Another indication might be that the person reports "people are taking my things" or "are out to hurt me." The homeless person often has their belongings stolen and have frightening events. The worker needs to distinguish if the person's paranoia is a symptom of a disorder or is simply a healthy protection from the real dangers of the street. The worker does not confront the paranoid suspicions. The worker initially tries to form a relationship rather than trying to convince the person there is no apparent basis for their suspicions. Depending on the degree of paranoia, the person's tolerance for interaction with others varies. The homeless person with paranoia often feels safer in a hotel room than in a shelter. The paranoia may be so great that fear of snakes and smells can drive the person from their housing and keep them outside if there is no psychiatric intervention. In relating to those suffering from paranoia, the worker needs to be careful not to make quick movements because these may frighten the person.

The homeless person with paranoia frequently cannot trust enough to agree to immediately meet a psychiatrist or take medication. Ordinarily, the worker must slowly build the bond of trust as described in Chapter 2. If the worker meets their needs as the person requests them, this bond of trust may be built. Getting to know the distinguishing features of the person's trust issues can assist the worker to help the person meet certain needs even when the person is not on medication. This often takes much patience, knowledge of the person, and creative strategies.

For example, a person with a paranoid disorder may not be able to deal with the necessary agencies to receive their disability payments. But if the person trusts a worker, in time, the fearful person might sign a form to give that worker authority to act in the person's name and get their Social Security or welfare check.

The ability of the person disturbed by these inner experiences to take care of their basic needs varies. The worker might have to assess to determine whether the homeless person needs to be placed under a conservatorship, that is, helped against their own will by order of a law court. To assess for the need for a conservatorship the worker can ask themselves the following questions:

> Can the person obtain food and clothing for themselves and protect themselves from dangers?
> Can the person get help if they have life-threatening health problems?

If the person is not able to take care of their needs and this is provable, the person can be forced to receive help, that is, to be conserved. If the present situation is life-threatening, an ambulance must be called. The worker needs to explain the inability of a person to care for themselves. The worker can help this process by following up with a call to the emergency room and again sharing significant information with hospital staff who are making the assessment to document that the person cannot care for themselves .

In a few cases, the homeless person with a mental disorder is not able to take care of their needs, but the danger is not imminent. If there is a caring, responsible family member and clear medical and social work documentation, then the worker can encourage the family to obtain conservatorship through the probate court. I found that often the family members of a homeless person with a mental disorder were unaware or were in denial about the present circumstances and the degree of danger to their kin. The relatives also felt reluctant to go against the wishes of the homeless family member. I had to educate the relatives to the real risks of the situation and to spell out the results that were likely to occur if the conservatorship did not take place.

If there is no family member who is willing to be the conservator and the person does not have an income that can pay a conservator, it is sometimes extremely difficult to get the necessary assistance, especially for the paranoid person who flees contact. Frequently, the physically strong person with the disorder of paranoia stays on the street until a life-threatening circumstance happens. It is important for the worker to always stay open to the person and to maintain contact because when a health problem does occur, then the person might turn to the worker's agency for assistance.

The following incident relates a first attempt to house a person with severe paranoia:

> A very sweet, frail man named Mike told me a sad story about his son and wife doing strange things that threatened his well-being. Mike felt he had to move and to keep his whereabouts secret. In this first case, I must admit that I took Mike's story at face value. I went to much trouble to help him make a financially costly move to a senior building. Within a few days, Mike reported

> people were doing strange things to him. Mike said he had to sleep on the closet floor to be safe. I feared for his health because he said he had recently had delicate heart surgery. Mike also talked about people poisoning him, so he did not eat well. Before long, Mike checked himself into a downtown slum hotel. Even though Mike was neat and clean, had a remarkable memory, and presented himself as very much together, his paranoid flight put his fragile health at risk. Through a combined effort by the family, our agency, and the county senior psychiatric outreach worker, Mike was put under a conservatorship and taken to a psychiatric hospital. After a few weeks on medication, Mike was able to live with his family. The family was cautioned to administer Mike's medication to him and to make sure it was swallowed. Our agency followed up with the family for several years.

Delusions. A person with a mental disorder may experience fearful beliefs that are limited to a certain area of their lives. It causes them discomfort but also can make them feel special. With strong support this person might be able to get housing:

> Marie experienced people's putting dust in her clothes. She was living with a friend, so when she applied for senior housing and reported this, she discovered that she was not accepted. At the next place she applied, she decided not to talk about these thoughts. She continued with some strange behavior, but it is tolerated. Marie was able to live an ordinary life in a senior residence and keep in contact with her family.

Schizophrenia and Seniors

Seniors who have schizophrenia may not be properly diagnosed because, with the aging process, some symptoms often become milder. The voices may lessen and the thinking seems clearer. Still, in listening carefully to the homeless senior, the worker has the sense that the pieces do not exactly all fit together. If the worker notes that the person was not able to work or maintain relationships in the past, this points to possible schizophrenia.

Mood Disorder

Depression is common among the homeless. The losses leading up to homelessness and the state of homelessness contribute to the depression. Depression can cause sleeplessness, an inability to concentrate and to make decisions, and a lack of energy to move their lives forward. A person suffering from severe depression needs a psychiatric evaluation and treatment and may benefit from medication. For some persons, depression may be so severe that they are suicidal. Chapter 3 provides the worker with questions to assess the level of the danger of suicide.

Another mood disorder is *manic-depression,* also referred to as bi-polar disorder, in which the person experiences mood swings. When manic, the person becomes very active and can spend all their money rashly. A few weeks later, the person can have a depressed mood with suicidal thoughts. This person needs to be under psychiatric care and usually is prescribed lithium, a drug that requires close monitoring by a physician because too high a level can be very dangerous. Lithium cannot be mixed with alcohol use. In assisting the person with a manic-depressive disorder, it is *critical* that the worker be vigilant to two factors: the medication is being taken as prescribed and regular medical check-ups take place. The worker needs to take special care that the person's placement provides watchfulness of the person's medical needs, yet gives as much personal freedom as possible. This watchfulness allows the person's life to remain stable.

> Fannie was a 70-year-old woman who told us she was a famous actress. She would come in dressed extravagantly, and she talked incessantly. She would let us assist her with housing but watched closely so that she kept control of her money. At the beginning of the month when her disability check came, she insisted she just had to leave town because she had a wonderful opportunity in a neighboring state. In the middle of the month she called in a very depressed mood and asked for assistance to return to town. When she did return, she told how she nearly committed suicide. Fannie was stabilized by being under consistent psychiatric and medical care with the prescribed lithium and by money management.

Anxiety

The emotional disorder of *anxiety* causes a great deal of inner suffering. This can be manifested in phobias, panic attacks, and obsessive-compulsive actions. A number of seniors become homeless because of compulsively collecting items and literally packing their housing to the ceiling. This probably catches up with seniors more than younger persons because the seniors are not physically able to move the items they collect when a housing inspection occurs. Staying in contact with the senior until the problem gets the person into a crisis allows the worker to assist the person in the crisis. To obtain housing that somehow limits the person's possibility of collecting to a danger point is a difficult but a possible solution. For example, senior housing that has weekly housekeeping or periodic inspections may help keep the compulsion under control. This arrangement requires a good working relationship with the person with the compulsion.

Posttraumatic Stress Disorders which result from experiences of trauma, such as war, incest, or rape are common among the homeless. Homelessness itself frequently causes trauma. Treatment and a safe supportive environment are needed. I found that support groups of other homeless persons' sharing their experiences seemed to help the seniors overcome their traumatic experiences.

Personality Disorders

A homeless person can have personality problems that make it difficult for them to interact with others and keep their lives going forward. The worker needs to look for patterns of behavior that can lead the person into trouble. Understanding these patterns allows the worker to adapt or attempt to motivate the homeless person to modify their actions:

> Joan was a 55-year-old woman who was raised by an alcoholic father who abused her. Joan would arrange to buy second-hand cars from unsuspecting friendly people. After she received the car, Joan refused to complete the payments unless she was forced by legal means. Because of traffic violations she lost her driver's license a number of times but did just what was necessary to get it back. She would always try to avoid paying her last month's rent. She tried never to be alone; if one man died then

within two weeks she would go back to a previous relationship. She would refer to these older men as "daddy." Joan would let homeless men stay with her who often took advantage of her. She came to St. Mary's when she could not find housing. After assisting her several times and realizing that Joan did not follow through on the rental agreements, we set definite guidelines so that we would not be manipulated by her. We were emotionally supportive but stated very clear guidelines, such as, "If you want housing, you need to do this ...."

Cognitive Disorders

The thought processes of a person can be limited because of brain injury from a blow, a lobotomy, a stroke, Alzheimer's disease or long-sustained use of alcohol or drugs. The person's ability to make decisions and to take care of personal needs and finances are limited. In severe *alcohol dementia* there is a loss of short-term memory though the person can still remember the past. If the dementia is extreme, the person can still fixate on alcohol yet not have the cognitive ability to make a decision not to drink. The person with alcohol or drug dementia who receives a check without money management may be at high-risk to end up dead on the street.

Jim was a 70-year-old man who survived on the street because once a month an old friend looked him up and helped him get clothing and cleaned up. Jim ate once a day at the St. Vincent's dining room. After six months of contact with a worker from St. Mary's, Jim asked to be housed. The worker placed him in temporary housing. Jim was in total denial about his drinking. He panhandled a few coins, and every cent went to alcohol. Sometimes the worker gave him a few dollars to wash his clothes. Although over and over again he said that he would use the money on washing clothes, he never did. The worker realized that Jim was not able to care for his personal hygiene without someone else's washing his clothes. When Jim received cognitive testing, it showed that Jim had excellent memory of the past, but his memory of the present was sketchy. Jim's ability to make decisions was also severely limited, therefore, he was not able to make a decision not to drink. A few times Jim received a small check and then drank until the money was all gone. Because Jim trusted the worker, he was able to tolerate money management. He came to the Drop-in Center daily, enjoyed the company of the other seniors, and was able to live quite independently in a senior hotel that provided two meals and housekeeping.

Rufus was a 70-year-old homeless man who had *cognitive impairment from a stroke*. It took time to build a relationship and to assess why he had a lack of funds for housing. A local woman who was a drug user fed on Rufus' loneliness. She conned him for money for "schooling" and other projects. In time, Rufus confided that he had given the women and her friends all the money from the sale of his home—thousands of dollars. The same group then told him that he needed to give them more money to get his money back. Because of his impaired thinking, Rufus was susceptible to this manipulation. Because Rufus was a veteran, with some advocacy and support he was able to settle into the Veterans' Home away from the con artists. He visited St. Mary's Center for continued social support.

In a society those who are organically impaired are often considered persons who have nothing to give. I learned the deepest lesson about love and friendship from a man who had an organic impairment. The man was Lovie's friend John. There is a part of John's story (see Chapter 1, Lovie Burkes' Story) that the reader does not yet know:

John had a lobotomy early in his life, so at 68 years of age he had a limited ability to care for himself. John was a very kind man, whose compassion led him to reach out to Lovie and help save her life by sharing food and housing. But at the same time John was in danger himself. One day when he came to the office, we noticed that there were flies buzzing around the cap that John always wore. When we looked closely, we saw that he had lice in his hair.

A coworker Father Don Bernard and I visited John's substandard housing and discovered that it was lice-filled. We then made arrangements to move John to housing where some personal care was provided. But before he could be accepted, we knew that John would have to be free of lice. Father Don and I got some special medicated soap provided by the physician's assistant of the Over-Sixty Health Center and coaxed John to let us help him get ready for his new place. With special encouragement John let us take off his hat. There were visible maggots eating into his skull. We applied the soap. Later, Father Don taught John how to do his own personal care.

DUAL DIAGNOSIS

Dual diagnosis is a lay term used to refer to a diagnosis of both an addiction and another mental disorder. A person with a dual diagnosis can easily be homeless for a number of reasons. This double disorder makes the person very vulnerable. They cannot access services by themselves, and few services are available, though this is slowly changing. Often, the complex nature of their disorders is not correctly diagnosed. If they are not correctly treated, they will not be stabilized.

It is difficult to serve a person with a dual diagnosis because the double disorder is difficult to untangle. Its history is like the chicken and egg dilemma. That is, which came first, the addiction or the other mental disorder, and how do they affect one another? Did the addiction cause the mental disorder? Or, is the person who has a mental disorder trying to medicate themselves through using the addictive substance?

Often the worker is most challenged in assisting the dual-diagnosis homeless person. The worker needs to understand both the addiction and other mental disorders and to recognize the services needed by this person. Forming the relationship and inviting into the community may take a very long time. If the worker tries to obtain a conservator for the disabled person through the county services, they find that the department is overburdened and has a lack of resources.

The following story of JP who Mary's workers attempted to serve for three years showed this clearly:

> JP is a 55-year-old woman who was extremely paranoid and used all the money she could obtain for alcohol. When intoxicated, she was aggressive and severely misused any dwelling where she stayed. Therefore, she was mainly outside. She was also deaf which increased her paranoia. Anyone who talked to her had to stand a few inches from her ear. JP resisted any offers to assist her with medical or psychiatric care. She went from week-to-week between jail and the general hospital emergency room. Neither agency was willing to deal with her deeper problems. Because JP survived outside and resisted treatment, she had not been required to receive the psychiatric treatment that could stop the vicious circle. The worker hoped that one day JP would overstep her bounds and be put under conservatorship. Then she would be helped. Unfortunately, the worker feared JP might die from the effects of alcohol, lack of food, medical attention, and the ravages of the elements before she was helped. At the time of this writing, JP's situation has not changed.

Often with consultation, creative strategies, patience, skill, strong advocacy, and—if necessary—legal conservatorship, the dual-diagnosis person can be helped. The approach with the dual-diagnosis person is more supportive and less confrontational than with addiction alone. *Assessment and Treatment of Patients with Coexisting Mental Illness and Alcohol and other Drug Abuse*[21] is a good reference that explains dual diagnosis in detail.

An example of a person with a dual diagnosis being stabilized was Lovie Burkes. Lovie Burkes had an alcohol addiction and another mental disorder. Not only is it very narrow ground to walk on to bring the person with a dual diagnosis into recovery but the challenge is to maintain consistent support in order to provide ongoing stability.

SKILL BUILDING—Assisting those with mental disorders.

✓ Role play the following situations with 1) the homeless person and 2) the worker:

a) A worker assisting a homeless paranoid person on the street.

b) A worker relating to a woman with manic-depressive episodes who has lost her hotel room for the past two months because she has spent the money in a few short days.

c) A worker relating to a dual-diagnosis person who uses alcohol as medication to deal with hearing voices.

Discuss your feelings after the role play and problem solve together about what would have to happen to help the person become stable and stay stable.

✓ While respecting the anonymity of the person, workers relate difficulties they may be having in assisting a person with a mental disorder. Problem solve how to effectively assist the person.

WHAT WE ALL CAN LEARN FROM LOVIE BURKES' STORY

Lovie was a vibrant member of the St. Mary's community. She helped with the alcoholism meeting and often set up the room for the women's support group. She was a member of the peer board and an active participant in the weekly support group. Lovie often spoke to public groups telling bluntly of the horrors of the street and humorously of her alcoholism. True to her name, she had a steady love for her friend John.

Lovie reconnected in a strong way with her family, talking frequently to her daughter and three generations of relatives on the phone. On Christmas 1993, she flew to Youngstown, Ohio, for a week-long reunion. In June of 1994, Lovie left St. Mary's to start a new life with her family in Youngstown. When I called in October to talk to Lovie about this book, I discovered that Lovie was back at risk of being homeless again. Her daughter said she was almost ready to toss Lovie out. In listening to the daughter, I found out what had gone wrong:

Before Lovie returned to Ohio, she appeared so capable that her new caseworker who had only seen the stabilized Lovie sent her home to Youngstown with an extra prescription. The daughter, too, did not realize the potential danger because Lovie seemed so independent. Also it took several months before the daughter was able to help Lovie receive her SSI check or healthcare services in this new state. She ran out of medicine, and the prescription needed to be renewed. Lovie again reported hearing strange voices. The daughter did not know the danger signs. Soon Lovie traveled to the grocery store to get a beer. She found a bar she went to without telling her daughter.

When I called, Lovie was in total denial. Her daughter told me she called the psychiatric hospital for assistance. They told the daughter to bring Lovie into the emergency room. Because of her paranoia, Lovie would not do this willingly, and the daughter was afraid of trying to force Lovie and losing their new found trust. St. Mary's caseworkers became involved. They contacted Adult Protective Services in Ohio. Lovie's daughter tried to follow through, but Adult Protective Services, the mental health center, and the probate court each told her the other would have to assist Lovie. St. Mary's staff had to again intervene and advocate by calling these agencies. With supportive counseling, the daughter was able to sign a form from the probate court which then acted quickly (not the case in some states). Lovie was taken against her will to the psychiatric hospital. A third time St. Mary's had to advocate so that Lovie could stay long enough to be fully stabilized.

This is a clear example of how the lack of a nationwide network of social services caused by their dismantling in the '70s effects those with mental disorders and their families. There are very few case managers to keep the person stabilized, especially when a disabled person moves. This demonstrates how the present system cannot respond effectively to the family member. In addition, the person with a mental disorder is even more unable to access the system before their precarious balance is destabilized, and they spiral down to the streets. This lack of a safety net is ineffective and cruel to the frail and deprives the person and the community of the richness of the character of the person involved.

THE WORKER IS SAVING THE WHOLE WORLD

The worker with the homeless is normally paid poorly and has a stress-filled, nearly impossible task. The worker is doing the most human act any of us can do which is to love, and they give that love by giving the homeless person what they need to live. As in the recent movie *Schindler's List* the quote from the Koran: "To save one life, is to save the whole world" applies. The worker with the homeless is saving the whole world.

I pray that more workers, volunteers, educators, national and state representatives and ordinary citizens will realize that we with resources must look beyond our narrow experience to those who need assistance. We need to realize the simple wisdom of the 80-year-old developmentally disabled senior who when his hotel was shut down could not find a new home. He said, "Sometimes we need a little help to help ourselves." We would all be wiser if we shared this vision.

SUMMARY

The worker's attitude of respect for the dignity of the person with a mental disorder allows the worker's relationship to be empathetic and empowering. If the worker examines their fears and stereotypes, their understanding of the person with a mental disorder increases.

Understanding the inner world of the homeless person with mental disorders allows the worker to be more effective in helping the person be stabilized.

The worker must recognize the special needs of those with mental disorders and learn to assist them to get their basic life necessities met and the psychiatric help necessary so they can keep permanent housing.

Dual diagnosis is a lay term referring to the person with an addiction and another mental disorder. For the worker to assist the homeless person with dual diagnosis takes more patience, energy, and advocacy.

The homeless person with a mental disorder can teach us great spiritual lessons of human love but may not be able to meet their own needs. A homeless person may only be able to share their gifts after they receive the help they desperately need.

The worker and any person who assists the homeless person to live is truly loving. The Koran statement applies to them: "To save one person is to save the entire world."

Christmas in the Streets of Oakland—Poem

Oh, light the tree with fireworks in the harbor.
Tinsel the street lamp.
Christmas is coming.
Hope, Love and Sharing are alive.

Old man dragging your belongings
  bagged as garbage,
  a Santa overloaded,
I know, old man, you carry your wine jug
  and your crumbs of food
  that you pull out on street corner.
Does Christ come for you?
Will you die soon struck down
  by train or car?

Philip is your name,
  spoken with Eternal Love
  by Creator Parent sixty years ago,
  and each moment with no less care.

Old woman, body-crammed
  in nightly doorway,
  seeking protection from the bay fog and frost and long winter
        rains,
Somewhere in the years
  genetics or environment
  brought too much to mind's synapses,
  and new routes fired.
Fear-driven thoughts and strange ideas jumble together.
Roof declared too expensive.
Food to eat seems only worthy
  your monthly check.

Lorraine, does your Creator love you?
Will Emmanuel be God with you?
I know young boys taunt you for play
  to hear your fear-raised curses.

As sure as Jesus told of Lazarus at the Feast,
  as sure as King slept in animal stall,
  as sure as Love died,
  spit-splatted, blood matted
  outside the city,
You, old man Philip
  and you "crazed" Lorraine
  are Christmas-ed each day.
Emmanuel abides in you,
  carrying your bag, O Philip.
  taking your taunts, O Lorraine.

Oh, inverted world, holding Spirit's secrets,
  Christmas upon me.
Penetrate my eyes unused to truth's paradoxes.
Star of David, enlighten my mind,
  wall-street crazed.
O pity me, who know not
  my bag of cumbrance
  or illusions of reality.
Jesus, come to me,
  that I may adore you
  in Philip's bleared eyes
  and Lorraine's fearful confusions.
Christmas me, O Emmanuel.

This was written in 1989. Since then after about 20 years on the streets Lorraine is safe, in a modern and well-staffed senior psychiatric nursing home. Our outreach worker discovered Philip attending a county fair, clean and well-cared for. God is good!

NOTES

[1] Lecture, Joan Chittister, OSB, Berkeley, 1993.
[2] St. Mary's Homeless Senior Program continues at this writing. Director, Susan Werner, St. Mary's Homeless Senior Program, 635-22nd St., Oakland, CA, 94612, 510-893-4723.
[3] General Assistance (GA) also called "welfare," is a County Social Service Assistance for those who meet requirements that vary from county-to-county but within state and federal guidelines. GA is for persons with limited resources and no, or very limited, income.
[4] A. De Saint-Exupery, *The Little Prince* (New York: Reynal & Hitchcock, 1943).
[5] C.R. Rogers, *Client-centered Therapy* (Boston: Houghton Mifflin, 1951).
[6] Lecture of Robert Titley, Ph.D., Colorado State University, 1972.
[7] D. Keirsey and M. Bates, *Please Understand Me* (Del Mar: Prometheus Nemesis, 1978).
[8] D.R. Riso, *Personality Types* (Boston: Houghton Mifflin , 1987).
[9] A board and care facility in California, is a state-licensed facility that provides housing, food, and medical needs for the disabled.
[10] *Confidentiality: A Guide to the Federal Laws and Regulations* (New York: Legal Action Center of the City of New York, Inc., 1991).
[11] J.J. English, *Choosing Life* (New York: Paulist, 1978).
[12] R.N. Bolles, *What Color Is Your Parachute* (Berkeley: Ten Speed, 1972).
[13] Lecture, J.C. Futrell, SJ, Denver, 1981.
[14] Social Security Supplemental Income (SSI) is an entitlement, mandated, and partially funded by the federal government. State participation is optional and requires a partial payment by the state. It includes financial and medical benefits for those disabled and elderly with no or limited income.
[15] *Federal Benefits for Veterans and Dependents*, (Washington, D.C.: Department of Veteran Affairs).
[16] Federal hearing on the Older Americans Act in San Francisco, 1993.
[17] The Holy Cross Associate Program is a student volunteer group that provides service for a subsistence stipend. The program is sponsored by the Holy Cross Community at Notre Dame, IN.
[18] Adapted from "The Art of Listening," *Stephen Ministries Training Manual* (St. Louis: Stephen Ministries, 1983).
[19] Another resource for working with homeless seniors is D.W. Burr and T.A. Rich (Eds.), *Old and Homeless* (Tampa: University of South Florida, 1993).
[20] *Diagnostic and Statistical Manual of Mental Disorders, Fourth Edition* (Washington, D.C.: American Psychriatric Association, 1994).
[21] *Assessment and Treatment of Patients with Coexisting Mental Illness and Alcohol and other Drug Abuse (*Rockville, MD: Center for Substance Abuse Treatment, 1994).

About the Author

M. Elizabeth Fuhr grew up on a farm near Bryant, South Dakota. She was the middle of the seven children of Etta and Robert Fuhr who were first educators and then farmers.

After high school Elizabeth became a member of the Third Order of St. Francis and St. Clare of Assisi at Marycrest, Denver, Colorado. She started her professional work as a high school science teacher. Then Elizabeth found her forte in creating programs that empower people to participate in their own education and healing. She developed a community-oriented model for a youth correctional ministry program in Colorado, a self-help grief program in northwest North Dakota, a church-based employment network in Littleton, Colorado, and recently a homeless senior empowerment program in Oakland, California. Presently Elizabeth resides in Denver. She is helping build a wholistic program that emphasizes the empowerment of women.

Elizabeth's education includes master's degrees in natural science, psychology and spirituality.

Elizabeth Fuhr can be reached at:

M. Elizabeth Fuhr
2851 W. 52nd
Denver, CO 80221
E-mail: mefuhr@aol.com FAX 303-433-5865
www.eoncity.com/mary

VIDEOS AND GREETING CARDS BY HOMELESS SENIORS

VIDEOS—FORMERLY HOMELESS SENIORS REVEAL THEIR STORIES: *VISIBLE LIVES*

Visible Lives (10 and 28 minutes) features interviews with formerly homeless seniors who speak of their previously hidden experience of being homeless and then the events that brought them to stability. The 28 minute video also presents the comprehensive case management and community program for homeless seniors at St. Mary's Center in Oakland, California, as presented in this book. Both videos were produced by Anne Sigler and released in 1996.

GREETING CARDS WITH ART BY HOMELESS AND FORMERLY HOMELESS SENIORS

Each pack contains 6 cards of different images and costs $10.00 (includes tax and shipping). Cards are blank on the inside. All art work was created by seniors at St. Mary's Center.

MASKS: Color photographs of masks in which seniors portray memories of their youth and aging with wisdom. Stories by the artists about their masks and lives are printed on the back.
NATURE ART: Water color paintings of a polar bear, a wolf, a turkey, a heart, trees, and teddy bears.

The proceeds support St. Mary's Center's programs to help seniors find housing and to stay in their homes, to teach preschoolers, and to feed hungry families.

Order Form—VIDEOS AND GREETING CARDS

		Number	Cost Each	
VIDEOS:	(10 Minutes)	________	@ $15.00	= $________
	(28 Minutes)	________	@ $25.00	= $________

Sales tax: Videos
7.25% for CA residents only except
8.25% residents of Alameda, Contra Costra, Los Angeles, San Mateo, and 8.5% for San Francisco or present tax rate = $________
Shipping: Videos 1-4 = $4.00 = $________
Subtotal = $________

		Number	Cost Each	
CARDS:	Masks	________	@ $10.00	= $________
	Nature Art	________	@ $10.00	= $________

Tax and shipping are included in cost of cards.
Subtotal = $________

TOTAL = $________

Name____

Address____

City________________State______________Zip__________________

Tel________________FAX______________E-mail________________

Mail check payable to: St. Mary's Center

Senior Services
St. Mary's Center
635-22nd St.
Oakland, CA 94612
TEL 510-893-4723 FAX 510-893-0119

Order Form—BOOK

NO PLACE TO STAY
A HANDBOOK FOR HOMELESS OUTREACH

Cost per Copy:	Number		Cost Each
	1–9	@	$10.00
	10–19	@	$ 9.00
	20–49	@	$ 8.00
	50 +	@	$ 7.00

Order:
Number of books ______ @ ________ Total __________

Sales tax:
7.3% For CO residents only or present state tax rate __________

Shipping:
Book rate:
$2.50 for first book and 50 cents for each additional book
Priority mail: $3.75 per book __________

TOTAL__________

Name____

Address____

City_______________State_____________Zip_________________

Tel_______________FAX_______________E-mail________________

Make check payable to:

M. Elizabeth Fuhr
2851 W. 52nd
Denver, CO 80221
E-mail: mefuhr@aol.com FAX 303-433-5865
www.eoncity.com/mary